How To Use
This Devotional Guide

This book is divided into 90 short devotional studies that slowly move through the Gospel of Mark. They are designed to be used one per day — but if your heart needs to spend a longer period of time with each study, you should move at your own pace.

Whether you have been following Jesus for a long time or have just begun your Christian walk, I hope this devotional guide will lead you to a deeper life in Christ.

Your daily walk will take the following pathway:

Read the Text — This study will take you through Mark's story of Jesus in 90 days. Begin each study by reading the portion of Mark for that day. It is printed in the study guide. You will probably want to use a marking pencil to underline words or phrases in the reading that speak especially to you. Read with an open heart and mind so that these words of truth begin to sink deep into your mind.

Think Through the Story — At the same opening as the text you will find a brief study guide. Even though your walk with Jesus is a very personal matter, this information (background material, word meanings, etc.) will fill in the gaps, giving you a more balanced walk through the Gospel of Mark.

Put Yourself in the Story — Each study also includes 5-10 thought questions. They are often very personal as they attempt to bring you into the story.

Record Your Conclusions And Decisions — The surest way to capture powerful thoughts is to write them down. A place is provided at each opening for you to record your conclusions and decisions from that day's devotional time.

Pray — Since prayer is the act of meeting God, there is a sense in which all you have been working through in each day's devotional is prayer. In addition to your prayer for the day, begin each week by completing the sentence, "My prayer for this week …." Put your personal goals down in prayerful words.

Summarize — The story of Jesus can be understood in terms of his relationships with followers, enemies, outcasts, and his Father — and also his relationship with you. At the conclusion of each week, summarize what you have learned about Jesus, about yourself, and about relationships.

Weekly Themes from the Gospel of Mark

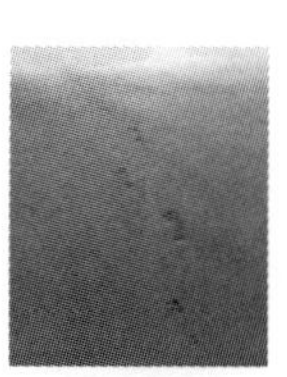

Day 1
1:1-8

Day 2
1:9-13

Day 3
1:14-20

Day 4
1:21-28

Day 5
1:29-34

Day 6
1:35-39

Day 7
1:40-45

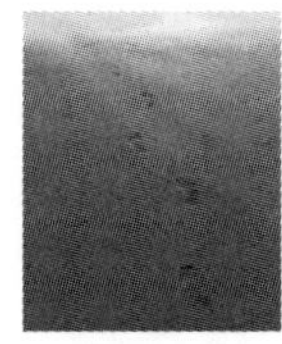

Week 1   *The Beginning*
Day 1-7   Mark 1:1-45

The Beginning

Mark 1:1-45

This week, as you walk with Jesus, you will be introduced to several of the major players in this powerful story: God, Jesus, the Holy Spirit, Satan and a few of the first followers of Jesus.

Try to put yourself into their time and place: to see with their eyes, hear with their ears, and simply follow along with the others as you begin this 90-day walk.

My Prayer For This Week …

Read Mark 1:1-8

For centuries the voice of prophecy has been silent. The Old Testament book of Malachi ended with mysterious words about a future forerunner (Mal 3:1; 4:5f). Now suddenly, in the desert where the Jordan empties into the Dead Sea, the voice of the prophet cries again. From the very beginning, John the Baptist plays the part of Elijah. He looks like that ancient prophet (2 Ki 1:8), finds a ministry in the same Jordan River area (2 Ki 5) and even plays the part of forerunner (Mk 9:11-13).

He has a message, but it is not one of abstract ideas or complex principles. Instead, his message is about a person — a person who is God incarnate. After all, history has been building to this climactic moment all along. If God is truly personal, then his clearest revelation of himself will be in the life of a person (cf. Heb 1:1-2).

1. Why is it "Good News" for God to become a person like us?

The life of Jesus Christ does not come as an unrelated event, but as the climax to a chain of events deeply rooted in history. In fact, all the prophets, from Moses through Isaiah to John the Baptist, have been helping to "prepare the way." And now John makes the final preparations:

Bad News — John prepares the way for Good News to be understood and accepted by highlighting the Bad News that exists in every human life. His focus on the bad news is clearly on target because it affects "the whole Judean countryside and all the people of Jerusalem" (vs. 5).

2. How would you define "bad news"?

3. How can facing Bad News prepare us to see Good News?

4. What is the general feeling about "sin" today? What is your attitude?

5. Why is it so difficult to admit our failures?

Good News — As much as John highlights the bad news of Sin, he also focuses on the good news of Forgiveness. This is why he is called "the Baptist," after his practice of washing and cleansing in the Jordan River "for the forgiveness of sins" (vs. 4).

6. Do you more easily focus on sin or on forgiveness? Why?

7. Why is repentance usually thought of in a negative way — "You had better change" rather than in a positive way — "You can change"?

His News — The "news" is about Jesus. So, John also prepares the way by personally staying out of the way. His humility is striking! At a time when it would be easy to encourage an unhealthy loyalty to himself, John points instead to Jesus:

> *"More powerful than I … I am not worthy" (Mk 1:7)*
>
> *"I am not the Christ" (Jn 3:28)*
>
> *"He must become greater; I must become less important" (Jn 3:30)*

8. What happens to the message when the messenger turns the focus on himself?

9. How can this happen today?

Mark 1:1-8

1 The beginning of the gospel about Jesus Christ, the Son of God. 2 It is written in Isaiah the prophet: "I will send my messenger ahead of you, who will prepare your way" 3 "a voice of one calling in the desert, 'Prepare the way for the Lord, make straight paths for him.'" 4 And so John came, baptizing in the desert region and preaching a baptism of repentance for the forgiveness of sins. 5 The whole Judean countryside and all the people of Jerusalem went out to him. Confessing their sins, they were baptized by him in the Jordan River. 6 John wore clothing made of camel's hair, with a leather belt around his waist, and he ate locusts and wild honey. 7 And this was his message: "After me will come one more powerful than I, the thongs of whose sandals I am not worthy to stoop down and untie. 8 I baptize you with water, but he will baptize you with the Holy Spirit."

My Thoughts Today ...

Read Mark 1:9-13 cf. Mt. 3:13-17

John is surprised when Jesus insists upon being baptized. After all, John's baptism was "for the forgiveness of sins" (vs. 4). So why does Jesus insist on being baptized by John (Mt 3:15)? It is true that, from this point on, Jesus will constantly identify himself with sinners — eating with them, traveling with them, sharing with them. And it seems very natural for him to identify so closely with them by submitting to baptism. But the fact remains that John is baptizing "for the forgiveness of sins." What in Jesus requires forgiveness?

In a very real sense Jesus knows that his baptism is for the forgiveness of sins — but not his own. He is already aware of the cross … moving toward it … committed to dealing with the plague of the human race — sin and guilt. But it is not his own failure that moves him on. It is a compassion that feels the pain of others. So, as he carries these thoughts with him into the Jordan, submitting to baptism, he rehearses the time that he will carry his cross and submit to death (cf. Mk 10:38; Lk 12:49-50).

1. Why are people baptized today? Why were you baptized?

2. How is baptism our re-enactment of the cross of Jesus (Ro 6:1-7)?

Jesus begins a mission that is both costly and very difficult. And it is at precisely this point that the Father voices three encouraging messages (vs. 10-11):

"You Are My Son" — We are a part of each other. It is clear that we are related because you are beginning a life of service to mankind just as I have been doing for centuries. Like Father, like Son.

"Whom I Love" — In your mission it will become clear that others do not love you, but I will never leave you. They will grow tired of hearing you, but my love cannot be exhausted. They will hurt you, but I will rescue you.

"With You I Am Well Pleased" — I am proud of you. I believe in you. You can fulfill your mission. The decision you are making, though very difficult, is exactly right.

3. What is it about Jesus' mission that brings this encouragement from God (see Php 2:7-11)?

4. Do you have a mission with God's stamp of approval? What is it?

Notice how the Father and Satan are both very active. As Jesus begins his ministry (Baptism), so Satan moves to stop him (Temptation).

5. How is this true in your own life?

Satan's attack is immediate. He cannot allow Jesus' ministry to succeed. His purpose has always been to oppose God's work, and Jesus represents the most comprehensive work God will ever do in human life. He must stop Jesus and he must stop him now.

6. What area of your life is the most vulnerable to Satan?

7. Why are there more people who believe in God's existence than there are those who believe in Satan's existence?

8. How is this a part of Satan's scheme?

Mark 1:9-13

9 At that time Jesus came from Nazareth in Galilee and was baptized by John in the Jordan. 10 As Jesus was coming up out of the water, he saw heaven being torn open and the Spirit descending on him like a dove. 11 And a voice came from heaven: "You are my Son, whom I love; with you I am well pleased." 12 At once the Spirit sent him out into the desert, 13 and he was in the desert forty days, being tempted by Satan. He was with the wild animals, and angels attended him.

My Thoughts Today ...

Read Mark 1:14-20

Six weeks have passed. For now the testing is over. Jesus is moving on to the task ahead. The forty-day testing period has clearly affected him. He is more certain of his mission, more decisive in his style. He enters Galilee with a clear purpose and a powerful message.

1. Does testing usually sharpen or weaken your faith? Why? How?

The forerunner has prepared the way. And now, the "one more powerful" (1:7) begins. But still Jesus shows the influence of John. Not only is he careful not to conduct his ministry in rivalry to John's, but he also reproduces John's message word-for-word (cf. Mt 3:1-2). His message is challenging:

"The Time Has Come" — Jesus knows that he comes from God (Jn 13:1). After 30 years of waiting, planning, preparing and, most of all, being away from his father, the time has finally come. He begins his work simply, slowly, solidly.

"The Kingdom Of God" — 13 times this phrase will come from the lips of Jesus (1:15; 4:11, 26, 30; 4:1, 47; 10:14, 15, 23, 24, 25; 12:34; 14:25). God is decisively entering into history. No longer will he rule through kings and political structures. Now, his offer is personal and direct. But, as the story unfolds, it will be very clear that this New message of the kingdom will have to contend with the Old.

"Repent And Believe The Good News" — More extensive than sorrow, deeper than a change of heart, the repentance Jesus calls for is a deliberate turning (Mt 13:15). When the kingdom of God becomes a reality there must be a new beginning, a change of values and conduct. Without the turning of a life, the "News" never becomes fully "Good."

2. Why are so many today unaware that "the time has come" in their lives?

3. What opposes the rule of God in human life today?

4. How can someone see, hear and understand, but still not turn?

It is significant to notice that as Jesus begins to choose the men who will form the base of his ministry, he does not go to a rabbinical school, but to the mainstay of Galilean society — the fishermen. Like the rest of the people of first century Palestine, they have long awaited a political Messiah. They want a warlord like King David to lead them against their Roman oppressors.

And so, at first, they follow Jesus for the wrong reasons . . . and he allows it! He knows that the old kingdom view will not easily give way to the new. He knows that the maturity of the disciples will take time and patience. But will they be as patient with him as the differences become clearer?

5. What in Jesus' message attracts you?

6. What in Jesus alarms you?

7. How have your reasons for following Jesus changed or matured?

8. How patient are you with those whose motives for following seem immature or even selfish?

14 After John was put in prison, Jesus went into Galilee, proclaiming the good news of God. 15 "The time has come," he said. "The kingdom of God is near. Repent and believe the good news!" 16 As Jesus walked beside the Sea of Galilee, he saw Simon and his brother Andrew casting a net into the lake, for they were fishermen. 17 "Come, follow me," Jesus said, "and I will make you fishers of men." 18 At once they left their nets and followed him. 19 When he had gone a little farther, he saw James son of Zebedee and his brother John in a boat, preparing their nets. 20 Without delay he called them, and they left their father Zebedee in the boat with the hired men and followed him.

My Thoughts Today ...

Read Mark 1:21-28

There was only one Temple. It was located in Jerusalem and it was a place of worship and sacrifice. But every Jewish community with at least ten families had a synagogue. They were scattered throughout Palestine and were places of worship, teaching, and instruction.

In Capernaum, on the northwest shore of the Sea of Galilee, the Sabbath-day synagogue observance followed a routine pattern. There were usually no surprises. But on this day, Capernaum's synagogue overflows with something new.

We do not know the content of Jesus' teaching, but we do know the impression it made. Notice that twice, the reaction to Jesus is the same:

To What He SAID (vs. 21-22) — "the people were amazed at . . . authority." The usual synagogue experience rarely went beyond a simple reading of scripture punctuated with quotes from famous rabbis of the past. Jesus refers to this procedure in his Sermon of the Mount:

> *"You have heard that it was said . . .Do not murder,*
> *and anyone who murders will be subject to the judgment."*
> *Matthew 5:21*

Here Jesus quotes one of the Ten Commandments (Ex 20:13) and the Rabbinical comment that, over the course of time, had come to be associated with it. But, both in his Sermon on the Mount and in the Capernaum synagogue, Jesus establishes his own authority. Rather than cite some human authority, Jesus speaks directly from God. This brings both excitement and hostility. Already the potential for jealously exists as Jesus is compared to the teachers of the law. But this is just the beginning of a rift that will only become deeper. It is the picture of both authentic and counterfeit religion, of both personal authority and borrowed authority.

1. How highly do you regard the religious "status quo" … the religious tradition of today?

2. Are you more impressed by opinion or scripture? Why?

To What He DID (vs. 25-27) — "the people were all amazed . . . authority." Jesus' power exceeds words — there is also action! And his action is so powerful and so good that there is an immediate recognition and response from the other side, the side of evil — "I know who you are . . ." (vs. 23). Jesus does not fit into any class of religious professional the crowds have ever seen. And so, it's no wonder they are amazed, or that the news about him spread, or that the professional religious community feels threatened.

3. What would change in your life and in your relationships, if what you said on Sunday, you did on Monday?

4. How would you contrast a life of active service with a life of religious talk?

21 They went to Capernaum, and when the Sabbath came, Jesus went into the synagogue and began to teach. 22 The people were amazed at his teaching, because he taught them as one who had authority, not as the teachers of the law. 23 Just then a man in their synagogue who was possessed by an evil spirit cried out, 24 "What do you want with us, Jesus of Nazareth? Have you come to destroy us? I know who you are — the Holy One of God!" 25 "Be quiet!" said Jesus sternly. "Come out of him!" 26 The evil spirit shook the man violently and came out of him with a shriek. 27 The people were all so amazed that they asked each other, "What is this? A new teaching — and with authority! He even gives orders to evil spirits and they obey him." 28 News about him spread quickly over the whole region of Galilee.

My Thoughts Today ...

Read Mark 1:29-34

Jesus quickly ("Immediately") moves out of the Religious Setting (the Synagogue) and into the Community Setting (Home & Street). It may sound wrong to contrast religion with community. But the kind of religion that Jesus is encountering is cut off from the community of people that he is making the focus of his mission.

1.   How has religion today isolated itself from the "real" community of people?

2.   What does religion lose when it moves away from its community?

The Home — After leaving the synagogue Jesus enters the house of Simon and Andrew. It seems that their house might be a rendezvous for Jesus and his disciples. Inside the home Jesus finds Peter's mother-in-law sick with a fever. Luke, the doctor, describes the situation more precisely. He says she "was suffering with a high fever." (Lk 4:38). It is possible that the fever is Malaria, which was common in the damp marshy flats around the lake. Jesus' reaction is characteristic of his style of ministry — He touches her. In the last incident (vs. 25), the power of Jesus worked through a word. But here it is action. He takes her by the hand and lifts her up, but no word is spoken.

3.   Why is personal contact so important in Jesus' ministry?

4.   What do you need and want when you are sick?

5.   How and why does your attitude change when others are sick?

This healing is immediate and dramatic. On one side of his touch there are burning cheeks, hot skin, dry throat, and sweating. On the other side of his touch every symptom is completely gone. Usually, after a fever breaks a person is still drained of strength. But not Simon's mother-in-law. Her energy level is high and her gratitude leads to service.

6.   What happens to gratitude if it is never expressed in service?

The Street — The power that fills the home soon spills out into the streets. It can not be contained. It can not be kept secret. A surging, growing crowd gathers outside. Mark describes the scope of the needs there and Jesus' response to them:

The Needs	*The Response*
"All who were sick" (vs. 32)	*"And he healed ... and cast out" (vs. 34)*
"Many who were sick" (vs. 34)	
"Various diseases" (vs. 34)	

The Sabbath — Even though the reports about Jesus are filled with hope and promise, still the people wait until the technical close of the Sabbath. Here is the "Lord of the Sabbath" (2:28), but they have yet to learn it.

7.   After a full day, what do you usually do after the sun sets?

The Demons — The same authority that awakens hope in the helpless (vs. 32-33) also brings a violent, convulsive confrontation with the demons (vs. 26, 34).

8.   Why is it significant that the demons know who Jesus is?

9.   What do they know and why doesn't Jesus want it told at this time?

Mark 1:29-34

29 As soon as they left the synagogue, they went with James and John to the home of Simon and Andrew. 30 Simon's mother-in-law was in bed with a fever, and they told Jesus about her. 31 So he went to her, took her hand and helped her up. The fever left her and she began to wait on them. 32 That evening after sunset the people brought to Jesus all the sick and demon-possessed. 33 The whole town gathered at the door, 34 and Jesus healed many who had various diseases. He also drove out many demons, but he would not let the demons speak because they knew who he was.

My Thoughts Today …

Read Mark 1:35-39

Throughout this first chapter there is a concentrated use of one of Mark's favorite words. He uses it to describe the pace of Jesus' ministry. It is the term "immediately." Although it occurs less than 10 times in the combined stories of Matthew, Luke, and John, Mark uses it no less than 42 times. Clearly Mark intends to show the urgent side of Jesus' ministry. Perhaps this is why Jesus has to get up "very early" just to have some special time alone with his Father.

As the story unfolds, it will become clear why this time is so important to Jesus.

1.   How far are you willing to go to find time alone with God?

2.   Do you have a plan?

At first glance, it might appear unusual that Mark's gospel focuses on three of Jesus' prayers (1:35; 6:46; 14:36-42). Of course these are not the only times that Jesus prayed. But the three times that Mark highlights are all moments of crisis in which Jesus uses prayer to make crucial decisions. In this first case, Jesus is faced with a difficult decision:

"Simon . . . Went To Look For Him" (vs. 36) — The word used to describe the search for Jesus is a strong one, meaning "tracked down." In fact, all occurrences of this term in the gospel of Mark echo Satan's attempt to distract or change Jesus' picture of his mission (3:32; 8:11; 11:18; 12:12; 14:1, 11, 55). Peter is the one who voices the temptation here, as he will later (8:32-33).

3.   How has Satan tried to change or distort the picture of what God says you can be?

"Everyone Is Looking For You" (vs. 37) — Clearly, Jesus is a local hero:

 "The people were amazed . . ." (vs. 21)
 "The people were all so amazed . . ." (vs. 27)
 "Evil spirits . . . obey him" (vs. 27)
 "Took her hand and helped her up" (vs. 31)
 "Jesus healed many . . ." (vs. 34)

Word spreads quickly. Everyone is talking about this Jesus! In fact, everyone is looking for Jesus — to find healing, to be taught, or perhaps, to simply thank him. The temptation is clear — Will he continue in the mission of his father? Or will he choose to avoid his hostile future by remaining a Galilean hero — accepted, appreciated, celebrated?

4.   What is happening in a person's life when the desire for "popularity" begins to play a major role in the person's decisions?

5.   What is the difference between wanting a "good reputation" and wanting fame?

"That Is Why I Have Come" (vs. 38) — Jesus went beyond making requests in prayer. He also made decisions in prayer. And so, here in Galilee, popularity loses to obedience. Jesus makes his decision. Immediately the pace resumes.

6.   How do you make decisions: impulsively, fearfully, prayerfully?

7.   Take time now and use prayer to decide the course of your day.

Mark 1:35-39

35 Very early in the morning, while it was still dark, Jesus got up, left the house and went off to a solitary place, where he prayed. 36 Simon and his companions went to look for him, 37 and when they found him, they exclaimed: "Everyone is looking for you!" 38 Jesus replied, "Let us go somewhere else — to the nearby villages — so I can preach there also. That is why I have come." 39 So he traveled throughout Galilee, preaching in their synagogues and driving out demons.

My Thoughts Today …

Read Mark 1:40-45

Jesus has prayerfully made a decision not to limit his ministry. God's mission is as broad as the human race and as particular as human failure. This decision is immediately tested:

"If You Are Willing" (vs. 40) — This leper is clearly desperate for recovery. His disease has excluded him from the general population and he is considered by the rabbis to be a living corpse.

1. What would a lifetime of rejection produce in a person's life?

2. How can this be reversed?

"I Am Willing" (vs. 41) — It is not unusual to feel pity. But Jesus is not just filled with pity. He also takes the unheard-of step of actually stretching out his hand and "touching" the man. It is unheard of ... for all except Jesus. His willingness to touch is simply a physical expression of God's desire to bridge the gap that the human race can never close on its own. Jesus sees touching as a vital part of his mission (1:31; 3:10; 5:27, 41; 6:5, 56; 7:33; 8:23, 25; 9:27, 36; 10:13, 16; 14:3). And although it brings criticism from his religious opponents (cf. Lk 7:39), Jesus continues to touch because compassion is not just something you Feel. It is something you Do.

3. Describe the power of the human touch.

4. What is the meaning and effect of withholding touch?

5. Think of someone you know who wears the scars of leprosy — the social leper who is excluded, unwanted, rejected, isolated.

6. How can you demonstrate the words of Jesus "I am willing"?

"Show Yourself To The Priest" (vs. 44) — Jesus is certainly aware of the various laws of "uncleanness." He knows that his touch makes him ceremonially unclean and puts himself outside respectable Jewish society. But he is also aware that the priests define "Clean" broadly and often used the term "Leper" to exclude those with any kind of skin problem or deformity. While the Law can protect the community from the leper, it can offer no help to the leper. So, what the Law cannot do, Jesus does.

7. Why do churches often design a benevolent ministry to protect members From, rather than to involve them With the outcast?

8. How are the two approaches different?

Jesus has a strange lack of concern for fame and prestige (vs. 43-44; cf. also 1:34; 3:12; 5:43; 8:30). Could this be a measure of authentic religion?

9. How could Jesus avoid crowds and yet attract them?

10. What happens to ministry when we focus on "image"?

40 A man with leprosy came to him and begged him on his knees, "If you are willing, you can make me clean." 41 Filled with compassion, Jesus reached out his hand and touched the man. "I am willing," he said. "Be clean!" 42 Immediately the leprosy left him and he was cured. 43 Jesus sent him away at once with a strong warning: 44 "See that you don't tell this to anyone. But go, show yourself to the priest and offer the sacrifices that Moses commanded for your cleansing, as a testimony to them." 45 Instead he went out and began to talk freely, spreading the news. As a result, Jesus could no longer enter a town openly but stayed outside in lonely places. Yet the people still came to him from everywhere.

My Thoughts Today …

What I Learned This Week ...

... About Jesus

... About Ministry

... About Myself

Day 8
2:1-12

Day 9
2:13-17

Day 10
2:18-22

Day 11
2:23-28

Day 12
3:1-6

Day 13
3:7-12

Day 14
3:13-19

Week 2   *The Twelve*
Day 8-14   *Mark 2:1-3:19*

The Twelve

Mark 2:1-3:19

This week, as you walk with Jesus, you will see him choose his Apostles. But they are not the socially elite or politically connected. They are not the ones who would be chosen today. Instead, they are lower- to middle-class men. They come as followers with both serious problems and great potential.

In your mind, try to picture yourself following along as number thirteen.

My Prayer For This Week …

Read Mark 2:1-12

In this story of compassion and forgiveness is a battle that both disappoints and angers Jesus. His growing conflict with the religious establishment comes directly from his desire to help the sick and diseased. Eventually, it will be this conflict that will motivate Jesus to retreat to the Galilean shoreline.

1. Have your efforts to help ever brought you trouble?

2. How did you (or would you) handle it?

3. Did the experience move you closer to God? How? Why? Why not?

Jesus feels the press of the crowd. Some are curious or even afraid. Others are desperate.

Four Friends — As Jesus is preaching there is a sudden interruption. An insistent faith breaks through the layers of brushwood and mud, opening a hole above him. It is an aggressive, almost pushy faith that Jesus later praises in parable (Lk 11:5-8; 18:1-8). When Jesus sees that what brings the shower of dirt down upon him is the selfless faith of four good friends, his heart is filled with great joy, even though conflict is imminent.

4. How does this story redefine the meaning of "friendship"?

5. What moves the compassion of these four friends beyond feeling to action?

6. Why does real faith always express itself (Jas 2:14-26)?

Forgiven . . . Healed — There are two things wrong in this man's life — he is paralyzed, and he is guilty. Jesus responds without hesitation to the most important need — "your sins are forgiven" (vs. 5). Once again, Jesus' compassion for the man overlooks the threat of conflict.

7. Why did Jesus act first to replace guilt with forgiveness?

8. Is it easier today to focus on physical needs or spiritual needs?

9. Do you see your greatest needs as physical or spiritual? Why?

Which Is Easier — Forgiveness always threatens any purely legal system because it offers human failure mercy rather than punishment. So, when the teachers of the law hear Jesus offer forgiveness, they face two alternatives: They must oppose Jesus and his forgiving style, or they must humbly join the paralytic in admitting their own desperate need for forgiveness. They choose to oppose Jesus.

10. Why is it so difficult for us to admit our own guilt?

11. What is the real power of forgiveness?

Jesus turned to these religious professionals and asked:

"Which is easier: to say. . .Your sins are forgiven' or to say 'Get up. . .and walk'"

Actually both are difficult. We like to think that healing is more a work of God than forgiving, but both display the kingdom. And both threaten a religion that is more interested in power than people.

12. What is the appeal of "power"?

13. Are you more drawn to "power" or to God?

1 A few days later, when Jesus again entered Capernaum, the people heard that he had come home. 2 So many gathered that there was no room left, not even outside the door, and he preached the word to them. 3 Some men came, bringing to him a paralytic, carried by four of them. 4 Since they could not get him to Jesus because of the crowd, they made an opening in the roof above Jesus and, after digging through it, lowered the mat the paralyzed man was lying on. 5 When Jesus saw their faith, he said to the paralytic, "Son, your sins are forgiven." 6 Now some teachers of the law were sitting there, thinking to themselves, 7 "Why does this fellow talk like that? He's blaspheming! Who can forgive sins but God alone?" 8 Immediately Jesus knew in his spirit that this was what they were thinking in their hearts, and he said to them, "Why are you thinking these things? 9 Which is easier: to say to the paralytic, 'Your sins are forgiven,' or to say, 'Get up, take your mat and walk'? 10 But that you may know that the Son of Man has authority on earth to forgive sins . . . ." He said to the paralytic, 11 "I tell you, get up, take your mat and go home." 12 He got up, took his mat and walked out in full view of them all. This amazed everyone and they praised God, saying, "We have never seen anything like this!"

My Thoughts Today …

Read Mark 2:13-17

The Romans gave the job of collecting taxes to wealthy citizens. These citizens would, in turn, give the actual work of collecting the taxes to "tax collectors" — Jews who had sold out to the Romans. Corruption was common and most of the tax collectors were hated by the general Jewish population.

The Man — Levi conducts his tax collecting business at a toll-house on the road from Damascus in the north, down through Capernaum and on to the Mediterranean Sea. His second name, Matthew, means "the gift of Jehovah" but to most, he is not thought of as a gift but a scourge. Jesus, however, looks deeper into the man. He finds one who is tired of corruption and who longs for change.

1. Why does religion today often look to the rich for its leaders?

2. How can wealth become a spiritual barrier?

The Call — Like many living in Capernaum, Levi has many occasions to hear Jesus preach about a coming kingdom. He has probably also witnessed his miracles. But his decision to "follow" and leave his lucrative career guarantees him unemployment. For others, there is always fishing to return to, but for Levi, there is no turning back.

3. Why does the call of Jesus demand a "clean break" with the past?

4. Why will it be awkward for Jesus to have Levi following him?

5. Why did Jesus consistently work with every level of society?

The Meal — Levi wants Jesus to know his friends, but what a group!

Tax Collectors — They are thought of as overindulgent, immoral traitors. And while this is not far from the truth, it is not the only time Jesus risks sharing a meal or a conversation with tax collectors (Lk 15:1-2; 19:1-10).

Sinners — This is a technical term referring to those who fail to comply with the Pharisaic view of the law (Jn 7:49). It also includes those who live immoral lives (Lk 7:37, 39).

6. What made such people want to share meals with Jesus?

7. What happens to us when our chief concern is our image?

8. What happens to others when our chief concern is our image?

The Mission — Notice that when questioned by the religious leaders, Jesus answers with sarcasm. He says, in effect, that he did not come to call those who Think they are "righteous" but those who Know they are not. Health will only come to those who know and admit they are "sick." Jesus describes his ministry as a calling … an extending of invitations. Invited are those who know their own spiritual destitution. Not welcome are those enamored with their own goodness.

9. How do we usually respond to someone's admission of failure?

10. Why is it so difficult for us to "face" our own failure?

11. At what point do you conclude that someone is beyond hope?

13 Once again Jesus went out beside the lake. A large crowd came to him, and he began to teach them. 14 As he walked along, he saw Levi son of Alphaeus sitting at the tax collector's booth. "Follow me," Jesus told him, and Levi got up and followed him. 15 While Jesus was having dinner at Levi's house, many tax collectors and "sinners" were eating with him and his disciples, for there were many who followed him. 16 When the teachers of the law who were Pharisees saw him eating with the "sinners" and tax collectors, they asked his disciples: "Why does he eat with tax collectors and `sinners'?" 17 On hearing this, Jesus said to them, "It is not the healthy who need a doctor, but the sick. I have not come to call the righteous, but sinners."

My Thoughts Today ...

Read Mark 2:18-22

Jesus' conflict with Judaism is growing. His first mistake was forgiveness (2:5-6), his second was compassion (2:15-17) and now he is faulted for his ritual. Think through the conflict and his amazing words and analogies:

The Fast — The only fast commanded by the Law was for the Day of Atonement Yom Kippur (Lev 16:29; Ac 27:9). But fasting was considered by some to be a sign of great spiritual commitment. And so, additional fasts were observed by the Pharisees (cf. Lk 18:12). In addition to this, fasting was also thought of as a good preparation for the coming of the Messiah. And so, if Jesus has any ambition to appear religious and committed, he should join in. But he doesn't! He has in mind a festival, not a fast. And, in refusing to fast, he is insinuating that the Messianic Age has already begun. The "bridegroom" imagery from the Old Testament portrayed God as the husband of his people (Hos 2:19; Isa 54:5; Eze 16:7ff). Jesus steps deeper into conflict by hinting that he himself is the Messianic Bridegroom.

1.   **What is the difference between External Ritual and Internal Faith?**

2.   **Reflect on the joy Jesus suggests — What are your reasons for joy?**

The Cross — The inevitable cross is always in the back of Jesus' mind. He knows that joy will one day be clouded by death. He knows that the time to mourn and to fast will come — when he is "taken" (vs. 20). He alludes to Isaiah 53:8.

> *"By oppression and judgment he was taken away"*

The context of Isaiah 53 pictures the violent death of an innocent man who willingly takes the curse and punishment of others.

3.   **How can Jesus have "joy" even in the face of death (Heb 12:2)?**

4.   **Describe a mindset that can help us choose joy in difficult times.**

The Patch — It would be a mistake to patch old jeans with a piece of new denim that still has a lot of shrinking to do. In the same way, fresh wine, which has yet to do its fierce fermenting and expanding, would rupture an old leather wineskin that has lost its capacity to stretch. Here Jesus targets a religion that has become rigid, unyielding and unable to receive the freshness that he is bringing. The antiquated forms of Judaism cannot harmonize with the Kingdom of God that challenges its purpose and direction.

5.   **What, in your life, has lost its ability to stretch and change?**

6.   **How has organized religion become cold, hard and sterile?**

The Point — For those willing to follow, Jesus is like a breath of fresh air. But for the rigid and self-righteous, he is explosive and dangerous.

7.   **How has Jesus been "fresh air" to you?**

8.   **What in you is rigid and hard and most likely to be torn apart?**

18 Now John's disciples and the Pharisees were fasting. Some people came and asked Jesus, "How is it that John's disciples and the disciples of the Pharisees are fasting, but yours are not?" 19 Jesus answered, "How can the guests of the bridegroom fast while he is with them? They cannot, so long as they have him with them. 20 But the time will come when the bridegroom will be taken from them, and on that day they will fast. 21 "No one sews a patch of unshrunk cloth on an old garment. If he does, the new piece will pull away from the old, making the tear worse. 22 And no one pours new wine into old wineskins. If he does, the wine will burst the skins, and both the wine and the wineskins will be ruined. No, he pours new wine into new wineskins."

My Thoughts Today ...

Read Mark 2:23-28

In the course of their traveling, Jesus and his disciples stop in a grainfield for some quick nourishment. Once again, controversy emerges. In the last story, Jesus evoked the Pharisees' hostility. Now he stirs their resentment into hate. He is determined that human life will win the priority test.

Faithful Rules or Petty Regulations — The Rabbis listed 39 different kinds of work forbidden on the Sabbath (see Shabbath 7. 2). These rules and regulations have accumulated over the course of time and have come to be regarded by the Pharisees as Law. This is why they accuse Jesus of "doing what is unlawful" (vs. 24). Four things are forbidden — reaping, winnowing, threshing and preparing a meal. And so, here in one event, the disciples break all four "laws."

1. What is the difference between human tradition and God's Law?

2. How do human rules change over time into infallible decrees?

The Law? — The Law (Lev 19:9,10; Dt 23:25) does allow the hungry to pick grain from the field of a neighbor. In fact, the Jewish farmers were to leave the corners and edges of their fields unharvested and available to the poor and those traveling. But the Pharisees, who just happen to be standing in the grainfield, judge Jesus and his disciples as lawbreakers because they not only pick the grain, but they also rub them in their hands. This they determine to be "harvesting," which is forbidden by the Law (Ex 34:21).

3. Why do some people not only expect but even hope that others make a mistake?

4. What motivates this kind of "watchdog" approach to religion?

The Real Law Breaker — In the minds of many, David was an ancient hero who could do no wrong. And so Jesus' reference to his failure, unlawfully eating consecrated bread (1 Sa 21:1-6), is not to justify law-breaking, but to point out the inconsistency of the Pharisees. David clearly violated God's Law. Jesus only ignores human tradition. So, who is the real "Law Breaker"?

5. What causes and motivates such "selective judgment"?

6. What is the first step toward more honesty and consistency?

The Purpose of the Sabbath — The Sabbath is only an event, a thing. But a person is a living soul. And living souls are not created to aid and benefit things and events. Instead, it is the reverse. To use the words of Jesus "The Sabbath was made for man, not man for the Sabbath." People are not to be prisoners or victims of Sabbath rules and regulations. In fact, the Sabbath was meant to save men from the intolerable seven-day work week by providing a time of rest, reflection and worship.

7. How does your observance of Sunday worship benefit you?

8. When is your time of rest and reflection?

9. Why must we see the purpose of God's Law before we are able to interpret or apply it?

23 One Sabbath Jesus was going through the grainfields, and as his disciples walked along, they began to pick some heads of grain. 24 The Pharisees said to him, "Look, why are they doing what is unlawful on the Sabbath?" 25 He answered, "Have you never read what David did when he and his companions were hungry and in need? 26 In the days of Abiathar the high priest, he entered the house of God and ate the consecrated bread, which is lawful only for priests to eat. And he also gave some to his companions." 27 Then he said to them, "The Sabbath was made for man, not man for the Sabbath. 28 So the Son of Man is Lord even of the Sabbath."

My Thoughts Today ...

Read Mark 3:1-6

This healing is the last of six other Sabbath healings reported in the Gospels (Mk 1:21-28; 29-31; Lk 13:10-17; 14:1-6; Jn 5:1-18; 9:1-41). We can already see how the conflict has grown from apprehension (1:22), to silent criticism (2:6-7), to open criticism (2:16), to direct confrontation (2:24) and finally to plotting (3:6). Jesus' future is unmistakably becoming more dangerous.

"Some Of Them Were Looking" — The term used to describe the careful way in which Jesus is watched means "to observe scrupulously," "to follow with unrelenting observation." Ironic as it seems, these Jewish religious leaders have already turned against Jesus. But they are, at the same time, very jealous of his popularity and authority (1:22, 27; 2:10). They are very interested enemies who, instead of coming to the synagogue to worship, have come to "watch" and "plot."

1. **Why was Jesus such a threat to the religion of his day?**

2. **How might Jesus threaten the religion of our day?**

3. **Why do people "come to church" today, if not to worship?**

"Which Is Lawful" — Once again Jesus confronts his critics with another of his unanswerable questions which, in effect, says:

> *"Since you say that you are so concerned about the Sabbath,*
> *what is the best way to observe this holy day?*
> *By desiring to heal, as I do,*
> *or by desiring to kill, as you do?"*

To heal or to kill — even today these choices determine the purpose and manner of our day to day. Of course the killing is more subtle today — killing someone's character or reputation. And the healing may be less spectacular — listening, loving, touching. But still the choices are the same.

4. **How can "killing" rise up in a heart that is made for "healing"?**

5. **Why should we be as cautious of religion as Jesus was?**

6. **Why did the religious leaders remain silent to his question?**

"Stubborn Hearts" — Jesus' determination to put people above things is earning him bitter enemies. Mark says that Jesus "looked around," an expression Mark uses several times through his story (3:34; 5:32; 9:8; 10:23; 11:11). This searching glance finds stubborn hearts and his anger flares, as it always does, in the face of insensitive moral blindness. Actually, anger is present twice in this story — from within Jesus, who came to "heal," and from within those who came to "watch." The important difference is in the "why" and the "how" of the anger.

7. **Do you usually get angry when someone else is wronged, or when you are wronged?**

8. **When is anger appropriate?**

9. **What makes a religious heart stubborn and hard?**

1 Another time he went into the synagogue, and a man with a shriveled hand was there. 2 Some of them were looking for a reason to accuse Jesus, so they watched him closely to see if he would heal him on the Sabbath. 3 Jesus said to the man with the shriveled hand, "Stand up in front of everyone." 4 Then Jesus asked them, "Which is lawful on the Sabbath: to do good or to do evil, to save life or to kill?" But they remained silent. 5 He looked around at them in anger and, deeply distressed at their stubborn hearts, said to the man, "Stretch out your hand." He stretched it out, and his hand was completely restored. 6 Then the Pharisees went out and began to plot with the Herodians how they might kill Jesus.

My Thoughts Today ...

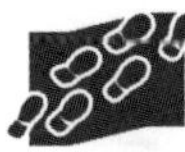

Read Mark 3:7-12

From the very beginning of his public ministry, Jesus has always had people around him. But here Mark shows that there is a big difference between a crowd of people and a group of disciples. All are invited, but only some are chosen.

1. **Sometimes today large religious crowds gather — why do they?**

2. **Some invest. Others only investigate. What's the difference?**

3. **In your own life do you only investigate, or do you finally invest?**

Jesus followed three stages:

Teaching — The small boat will be used more and more by Jesus and from now on it will take the place of the speaker's position in the synagogue. The language here is clear: "crowd followed" (vs. 7), "many people came" (vs. 8), "crowding him" (vs. 9), "pushing forward" (vs. 10). Jesus is at the height of his Galilean ministry. He is popular, sought after, a celebrity. People come from everywhere. Judea and Jerusalem are mentioned for the first time in connection with Jesus. Further south Idumea is mentioned and to the east the region of Perea, here described as "the regions across the Jordan." Also included is the northwest country around Tyre and Sidon. This is quite a diverse crowd.

4. **What is drawing all of these people?**

5. **What is overcoming their fear and prejudice as they mix and mingle with each other?**

Resting — Suddenly Mark introduces a new word, used only here in his gospel — "withdrew." This is a classical word found in Homer (withdrawing from battle) and Plato (retiring from public life). It shows that Jesus needs some time to himself. Whether it is the rising hostility of the Scribes and Pharisees, or just the need for rest, Jesus attempts to withdraw with his disciples.

6. **Why is time alone with God so important?**

7. **What happens in your life when you don't get it?**

It seems obvious that the presence of the crowd is no indication of their commitment. Crowds are always inevitable with any new religious undertaking. But a movement cannot be built upon the size of a crowd.

8. **How do a "crowd" and a "body" of Christians differ?**

9. **What are the dangers of staying hidden in the crowd?**

Choosing — At first there are "disciples" who "follow" Jesus. But now there are "apostles" chosen to "be with him." But notice that they are not chosen because of their great faith, which will waver, or their great talent, since none have unusual ability. In fact, all of them will desert, betray, or deny Jesus. But what they do have in common is their desire and willingness to go beyond following to being with Jesus.

10. **Describe the difference between following Jesus and sharing in His mission.**

11. **How is being "with" Jesus both a privilege and a responsibility?**

7 Jesus withdrew with his disciples to the lake, and a large crowd from Galilee followed. 8 When they heard all he was doing, many people came to him from Judea, Jerusalem, Idumea, and the regions across the Jordan and around Tyre and Sidon. 9 Because of the crowd he told his disciples to have a small boat ready for him, to keep the people from crowding him. 10 For he had healed many, so that those with diseases were pushing forward to touch him. 11 Whenever the evil spirits saw him, they fell down before him and cried out, "You are the Son of God." 12 But he gave them strict orders not to tell who he was..

My Thoughts Today ...

Read Mark 3:13-19

This is an important stage in Jesus' mission. Prior to this time, he has conducted his ministry in Galilean synagogues and in private conversations. But now, with growing controversy, the Jewish synagogues begin to close to him. And so, he chooses twelve men as the nucleus of his expanding ministry.

APOSTLE	DESCRIPTION	TEXTS
Peter	Impulsive and fearful at first	Mk 5:37; 8:29, 32-33
James	Angry, ambitious, and judgmental	Mk 3:17; 10:35-41
John	Quick tempered and ambitious	Mk 1:19; 10:35-41
Andrew	Excited introducer for Jesus	Jn 1:35-42; 6:8-9; 12:20-22
Philip	Doubted Jesus' feeding of the 5000	Jn 1:43-46; 6:5-7; 14:8-9
Bartholomew	Honest and outspoken	Jn 1:45-51; 21:1-14
Matthew	Dishonest and greedy at first	Mk 2:15-17; Lk 5:27-31
Thomas	Offered to die, but then doubted	Jn 14:5; 20:24-29
James	Identified with Cleopas	Lk 6:15; Ac 1:13
Thaddaeus	Also called Judas	Jn 14:22
Simon	Extremely patriotic – a Zealot	Lk 6:15
Judas	The only non-Galilean	Lk 22:47-48; Jn 12:4-8

1. **Why did Jesus choose only twelve?**

2. **What did Jesus see in these men?**

3. **Why would today's religious establishment probably disqualify them?**

4. **What kind of man would be chosen today?**

5. **What kind of person would be overlooked today?**

Jesus chose no priests or theologians. He chose no religious professionals. Instead, he chose lower to middle-class ordinary men. Whenever they are listed, they are usually divided into the same three groups:

The Strongest Leaders:

    Peter, James, John and Andrew.

The Reflective, Questioning Men:

    Philip, Bartholomew, Matthew and Thomas.

The Practical, Detail Men:

    James, Thaddaeus, Simon and Judas.

6. **Since Jesus knew what kind of man Judas was, or would become, why did he choose him?**

Mark 3:13-19

13 Jesus went up on a mountainside and called to him those he wanted, and they came to him. 14 He appointed twelve — designating them apostles — that they might be with him and that he might send them out to preach 15 and to have authority to drive out demons. 16 These are the twelve he appointed: Simon (to whom he gave the name Peter); 17 James son of Zebedee and his brother John (to them he gave the name Boanerges, which means Sons of Thunder); 18 Andrew, Philip, Bartholomew, Matthew, Thomas, James son of Alphaeus, Thaddaeus, Simon the Zealot 19 and Judas Iscariot, who betrayed him.

My Thoughts Today …

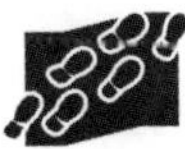

Week 2
What I Learned This Week ...

... About Jesus

... About Ministry

... About Myself

Day 15
3:20-21, 31-35

Day 16
3:22-30

Week 3   *The Kingdom*
Day 15-21   *Mark 3:20-4:29*

Day 17
4:1-2, 9-13

Day 18
4:2-7, 14-19

Day 19
4:8, 20

Day 20
4:21-25

Day 21
4:26-29

The Kingdom

Mark 3:20-4:29

This week, as you walk with Jesus, you will hear him teach about the Kingdom. He will use a two-pronged strategy.

First he aims at one of the greatest obstacles to his ministry — the popular political theories about the Kingdom that have existed for years. But then he also speaks directly to the Kingdom of the human heart and the need for God to rule there.

My Prayer For This Week …

Read Mark 3:20-21, 31-35

Imagine how Jesus must appear to his family and friends. Instead of settling down to an ordinary life following his father's trade, he becomes more and more involved with crowds, cures and suspicious company. A man who takes such an interest in unbalanced people must be a little off-balance himself. Notice that he is charged with insanity by both his friends and his enemies.

"His Family Heard About This" — No doubt the ones who are the most concerned are Jesus' family members since they "went to take charge of him" (vs. 21). The term "looking" (vs. 32) is the same one used to describe Peter's search for Jesus (1:36). It is a strong term implying that Mary is determined to "track down" Jesus. She is worried or upset or both.

1. How would you feel if your quest for God worried your family?

"Who Are My Mother and Brothers" — In his response, Jesus tries to be both kind and honest. Physical relationships do not always correspond to Spiritual ones. The natural ties of kinship do not carry any special claims or advantages. And for all the joy and privilege of being the mother of Jesus, Mary is still measured by the standard of God's will.

> *"Whoever does God's will is my brother and sister and mother."*
> *Mark 3:35*
> *"Blessed is the mother who gave you birth . . .*
> *He replied, Blessed rather are those who hear the word of God and obey it."*
> *Luke 11:27-28*
> *"You are my friends if you do what I command."*
> *John 15:14*

2. If "blood" is thicker than "water" — what would Jesus say is thicker than blood?

3. According to Jesus, who is in the "family" of God?

"The Will of God" — The phrase the "Father's will" occurs many times in the gospels (Mt 6:10; 7:21; 12:50; 18:14; 21:31; 26:42; Mk 14:36; Lk 22:42). And for Jesus, the "Father's will" is the center of his life:

> *"My food . . . is to do the will of him who sent me."*
> *John 4:34*
> *"I have come . . . not to do my will but to do the will of him who sent me."*
> *John 6:38*
> *"I do nothing on my own but speak just what the Father has taught me."*
> *John 8:28*
> *"The world must learn that . . . I do exactly what my Father has commanded me."*
> *John 14:31*

4. Why do we tend to be afraid of what family or friends think?

5. How did Jesus withstand the pressure?

20 Then Jesus entered a house, and again a crowd gathered, so that he and his disciples were not even able to eat. 21 When his family heard about this, they went to take charge of him, for they said, "He is out of his mind."

• • •

31 Then Jesus' mother and brothers arrived. Standing outside, they sent someone in to call him. 32 A crowd was sitting around him, and they told him, "Your mother and brothers are outside looking for you." 33 "Who are my mother and my brothers?" he asked. 34 Then he looked at those seated in a circle around him and said, "Here are my mother and my brothers! 35 Whoever does God's will is my brother and sister and mother."

My Thoughts Today ...

Read Mark 3:22-30

This is the last criticism from the religious leaders for a while. But it is designed to be one of the most damaging and Jesus takes it seriously.

Beelzebub — It is becoming absolutely clear that the religious leaders cannot deny Jesus' miracles and super-natural power as he heals the sick, casts out demons and overcomes evil. But, at the same time, they absolutely refuse to believe that his power is from God. Pride is their obstacle. They do not want to accept him as God's Messiah. So, they resort to innuendo and gossip.

1.   What is Jesus' attitude toward criticism of his ministry?

To say that Jesus is possessed by Beelzebub is really an insult. The term is a caricature of the word "Baalzebub" the "Fly-god" or the "Filth-god." It can be compared to today's cussing where, instead of using God's actual name, someone will use a form of his name. Beyond this, Jesus is accused of being in league with Satan since "Beelzebub," being an insult, was applied to Satan. These are serious accusations and Jesus takes them seriously.

2.   How does pride lead to recklessness, slander and violence?

3.   Why do many who say they seek God's truth actually resist it?

Two Parables — Jesus gives his reply in the form of two short parables:

· The Kingdom Divided — Satan is not a fool. He has a kingdom which, like all kingdoms, finds its strength in unity. Why should Satan raise civil war in his own kingdom?

· The Strong Man Bound — Rather than be a partner to Satan, the Messiah will tie up the strong man (Satan) and plunder his possessions. The Messiah is stronger than Satan. Every encounter with evil shows that Satan binds while Jesus frees.

4.   What impact is Jesus' reasoning having?

5.   Are stubborn hearts usually open to reason? Why or why not?

The Unforgivable Sin — This text has brought misunderstanding and pain to many who worry they have commit-ted the "unforgivable sin". But blasphemy against the Holy Spirit is not about a specific act of sin as much as it is about a general condition of the heart … a heart so diseased by evil that it cannot be forgiven. But this is not because God is not ready to forgive, but because the heart in question does not want forgiveness. It has taken evil so deeply into itself that repentance is not possible. This heart has hardened beyond the point of softening. If you are concerned about this condition, then you show that you are free from it, because the essence of this sin is its lack of concern, its callous blindness. If I stubbornly believe that evil is right and that good is wrong, God will not forgive because he will not force my heart to change. He will not deny me even my freedom to be wrong.

6.   How can a heart harden beyond the point of softening?

7.   Why would a person not want forgiveness?

8.   Thank God for his great mercy!

22 And the teachers of the law who came down from Jerusalem said, "He is possessed by Beelzebub! By the prince of demons he is driving out demons." 23 So Jesus called them and spoke to them in parables: "How can Satan drive out Satan? 24 If a kingdom is divided against itself, that kingdom cannot stand. 25 If a house is divided against itself, that house cannot stand. 26 And if Satan opposes himself and is divided, he cannot stand; his end has come. 27 In fact, no one can enter a strong man's house and carry off his possessions unless he first ties up the strong man. Then he can rob his house. 28 I tell you the truth, all the sins and blasphemies of men will be forgiven them. 29 But whoever blasphemes against the Holy Spirit will never be forgiven; he is guilty of an eternal sin." 30 He said this because they were saying, "He has an evil spirit."

My Thoughts Today ...

Read Mark 4:1-2a, 9-13

Jesus now begins to focus on one of the greatest obstacles to his ministry — the popular theories about the kingdom. Some are political. Others are material or religious. But they all oppose his attempt to communicate the real meaning of the kingdom — God's rule in human life.

1.   What ideas today wear the names of success, fulfillment, or accomplishment, but in reality oppose God's rule in human life?

2.   What is their appeal? How and why do they affect you?

Jesus enjoys telling stories because they create mental pictures that are easily remembered and become stepping stones to deeper truth. His stories parallel the familiar experience of rural life (farming, building, fishing) with the spiritual experience of God growing and shaping human character. Jesus is not the first to use parables. There are several in the Old Testament (2 Sa 12:1-7). Later Jewish writings contain similar stories. But the stories of Jesus are unrivaled, penetrating deeply into the hearts of those who gather to See, Hear, Understand and Turn for healing (Isa 6:10; cf. Mt 13:15).

But not every heart is open:

"Ears To Hear" — This phrase is a well-established part of Jesus' style (Mk 4:23, Mt 11:15; 13:9, 43; Lk 8:8; 14:35). It speaks directly to the real problem in communication — listening. Have you ever gazed deeply into someone's eyes and saw that the lights were on, but no one was home? Jesus has too.

3.   Contrast hearing with your ears and hearing with your heart.

4.   Think of your own experience with the Bible (reading, classes, sermons etc.).

5.   How deep does your hearing go … to your ears … to your mind … to your heart?

"The Secret Of The Kingdom" — Jesus' parables are not just teaching aids, like a chart or a diagram. They describe a "Kingdom" moving in a completely different direction and following a completely different purpose. This is why he calls it a "Secret." He knows that the deepest significance of God's kingdom will come only to those who have listened enough to come back for more. These are people who move beyond hearing the parable. In humility they take the next step. They begin to crack it open in search of the kernel.

6.   How can Jesus' words be amazing for some, puzzling for others, and life-changing for a few?

7.   Why is the truth concealed from the stubborn and hardhearted?

8.   Does God want it to be difficult to find?

"Don't You Understand?" — The teller of parables is important, but this chapter shows that the hearer really controls what happens to the message. The skill of the sower (God) and the quality of the seed (His Word) are infallible. Any problems that exist are with the soil (our hearts). We decide what to do with what we are hearing. It is our privilege and our responsibility.

9.   Ask God to till the soil of your heart, to make it soft and responsive.

10. Confess any hardness. Name it. Describe it. Ask for help.

1 Again Jesus began to teach by the lake. The crowd that gathered around him was so large that he got into a boat and sat in it out on the lake, while all the people were along the shore at the water's edge. 2 He taught them many things by parables …

• • •

9 Then Jesus said, "He who has ears to hear, let him hear." 10 When he was alone, the Twelve and the others around him asked him about the parables. 11 He told them, "The secret of the kingdom of God has been given to you. But to those on the outside everything is said in parables 12 so that, "'they may be ever seeing but never perceiving, and ever hearing but never understanding; otherwise they might turn and be forgiven!'" 13 Then Jesus said to them, "Don't you understand this parable? How then will you understand any parable?"

My Thoughts Today …

Read Mark 4:2-7, 14-19

The parable of the soils is a parable of hearing. It is surrounded and filled with a heavy concentration of discernment words:

vs. 2	He taught them many things by parables, and in his teaching said, "Listen!"
vs. 9	He who has ears to hear, let him hear.
vs. 12	They may be ... ever hearing but never understanding.
vs. 15	As soon as they hear it, Satan comes and takes away the word.
vs. 16-17	Others ... hear the word and at once receive it with joy.
vs. 18-19	Still others ... hear the word; but ... choke the word.
vs. 20	Others ... hear the word, accept it, and produce a crop.
vs. 23	If anyone has ears to hear, let him hear.
vs. 24	Consider carefully what you hear.

Unquestionably, agriculture is the best possible metaphor that Jesus could have chosen to describe the process of hearing God. The agricultural stories picture God penetrating deep into the soil of our lives, putting down roots and growing. They teach that we hear God with all we have made of ourselves — with every sin that we cling to — with all our worries, ambitions and desires. They all come with us to meet the message of God as it is read or spoken. And we respond to God with welcome or defiance — it all depends upon what we bring to the hearing.

There are not really four kinds of soils, as it seems, but only two — unproductive soil and productive soil.

Today consider three kinds of Unproductive Soil:

"Path" (vs. 4, 15) — Just as some seed will fall on the hard path that borders the field, God's seed (vs. 14) will fall on hard, inflexible hearts. Satan cannot take God's seed unless we allow it.

1. Why do we allow it?

2. What makes a heart hard?

"Rocky" (vs. 5-6, 16-17) — Sometimes seed will fall on a thin coating of soil where no depth exists. In a similar way God's truth sometimes appeals to our emotions but doesn't grip our conscience. So when the novelty wears off, we find that our shallow faith has no staying power.

3. What makes you want to quit? How can faith be deepened?

"Thorny" (vs. 7, 18) — Think of the common Arab weed nabk, which, when germinating looks very much like corn, but whose vigorous nature can eventually choke the life out of other plants. In the same way, the soil of our lives can become crowded with concerns that appear so large and occupy so much of our time that we lose the original impact of God's message. We become so busy living that we forget how and why we live.

4. What worries you the most? What worries you now?

5. How can these worries choke God's influence out of your life?

6. Ask God to soften, to deepen and to clean the soil of your heart. Ask him to prepare you to be productive soil.

2 He taught them many things by parables, and in his teaching said: 3 "Listen! A farmer went out to sow his seed. 4 As he was scattering the seed, some fell along the path, and the birds came and ate it up. 5 Some fell on rocky places, where it did not have much soil. It sprang up quickly, because the soil was shallow. 6 But when the sun came up, the plants were scorched, and they withered because they had no root. 7 Other seed fell among thorns, which grew up and choked the plants, so that they did not bear grain.

• • •

14 The farmer sows the word. 15 Some people are like seed along the path, where the word is sown. As soon as they hear it, Satan comes and takes away the word that was sown in them. 16 Others, like seed sown on rocky places, hear the word and at once receive it with joy. 17 But since they have no root, they last only a short time. When trouble or persecution comes because of the word, they quickly fall away. 18 Still others, like seed sown among thorns, hear the word; 19 but the worries of this life, the deceitfulness of wealth and the desires for other things come in and choke the word, making it unfruitful.

My Thoughts Today ...

Read Mark 4:8, 20

To conclude your look at the parable of the soils think about Productive Soil and consider the following guidelines for really hearing God (Mk 4:20; Lk 8:15):

Hear The Word — We must give the Word of God access to our hearts. Many view scripture as raw information, and they go to it to get data or facts. They see God's Word as columns of interesting information rather than a life-connection to God.

1. **What attitude and setting helps you to really "hear" the word?**

2. **Describe your life when you first encountered God's message.**

3. **How are you different now? How have you grown?**

Retain The Word — Once the Word of God touches our hearts and we begin to appreciate its story, we must then be willing to obey its truth. We must ask questions like: "What changes will this truth make in my life? How will it affect my relationships, my values and my purpose in life?"

It is challenging to discover that in the New Testament, the Greek words for "obey" (hypakouo) and for "hear" (akouo) share the same root. Since "obey" is derived from "hear," our faith has always been connected to hearing. "Faith comes from hearing the message" (Ro 10:17). Obedience sharpens our ability to hear and understand. The more we respond to God's story, the clearer it becomes. This is how we retain what we have heard. This is how faith grows. Obedience drives the hearing process deeper into our hearts.

4. **How do you measure spiritual productivity?**

5. **Why should "hearing" be followed with "obeying" in your life?**

Persevere With The Word — Just as soon as we make plans to retain what we hear, Satan makes plans to uproot what God is growing in our lives. So we must persevere. We must identify the areas in which we are most vulnerable. Worry, wealth and desires are among the tactics Satan can use to "choke the word" (vs. 19). Not using what we have been given (vs. 24) is another.

6. **Where does Satan attack you? What can you do? Who can you tell?**

Produce From The Word — There have been studies of the yield in Palestinian grainfields where ancient methods are observed. They show that a tenfold harvest is a very good yield, but the average is closer to about seven and a half. This means that, in Jesus' parable, a yield of thirty, sixty or one hundred times what was sown is not a normal harvest, but an extraordinarily fruitful one. His point is clear — This is a picture of God at work!!

7. **In this parable there is the Sower, the Seed, and the Soil. Of the three, where does the power to change reside? Who makes the decisions?**

8. **Look at your circle of acquaintances. Without prejudging them, what kind of soil do you see in their hearts?**

9. **How could you help them to become "good soil"?**

8 Still other seed fell on good soil. It came up, grew and produced a crop, multiplying thirty, sixty, or even a hundred times.

• • •

20 Others, like seed sown on good soil, hear the word, accept it, and produce a crop — thirty, sixty or even a hundred times what was sown.

My Thoughts Today …

Read Mark 4:21-25

Jesus continues to describe spiritual growth. Using a common object (a lamp) and a common place (a home), he takes the next step in developing the dominate theme of his teaching — the Kingdom of God. He builds on the parable of the soils, by moving from simply hearing the word (vs. 15, 16, 18, 20), to using the word, letting the kingdom shine. The two parables are connected with the repeated phrase:

"If anyone has ears to hear, let him hear."

While the imagery has changed from seeds and soil to light and lamps, the topic has not. Jesus continues to describe the power of God's rule in human life:

"Hidden" or "Disclosed" (vs. 22) — Like the parable of the soils, this is a parable about unused potential. If the light God shines in my life doesn't help other people to see, something is very wrong.

1.   What happens to your relationship with God when you hide it?

2.   Why is God's rule in your life supposed to be seen?

3.   What are appropriate and inappropriate ways for it to be seen?

"Concealed" or "in the Open" (vs. 22) — Notice how Jesus extends his explanation of the power of really "hearing." According to Jesus, hearing should bring discovery. To hear without discovery is like lighting a lamp and then covering it up with a bowl. God's Kingdom cannot be contained.

4.   Name the "bowl" that is most likely to cover your "lamp."

The lamp he mentions was at the very center of the Galilean home. Its purpose was to illuminate every part of the home. It was so central to the normal operation of the household that the people probably smiled as they imagined lighting their lamps and then putting them under a bowl or a bed. It didn't make sense.

5.   Describe how your life would change if the bowl was removed.

6.   Name one of the first steps toward removing the bowl.

"Ears to Hear" (vs. 24) — Beyond the discovery of the kingdom, Jesus enlarges his warning to include hearing without responding in obedience. To hear and not respond is to lose what we hear. Jesus is warning against inattentive listening. The penalty for such careless listening is an apathetic faith. What a frightening skill to learn … to grow immune to the kingdom. To hear without acting causes us to eventually lose our ability to understand spiritual truth.

7.   How can you consider more "carefully" what you hear?

8.   Describe the "measure" that has been given to you?

"Given more" or "Taken from" (vs. 25) — In spiritual matters standing still is impossible. We either gain ground or we give up ground; we advance or we decline in our spiritual understanding; we use it or we lose it.

9.   What do you hear from God? What responsibility does it give you?

10.   Why do we hide our true convictions about God from others?

21 He said to them, "Do you bring in a lamp to put it under a bowl or a bed? Instead, don't you put it on its stand? 22 For whatever is hidden is meant to be disclosed, and whatever is concealed is meant to be brought out into the open. 23 If anyone has ears to hear, let him hear." 24 "Consider carefully what you hear," he continued. "With the measure you use, it will be measured to you — and even more. 25 Whoever has will be given more; whoever does not have, even what he has will be taken from him."

My Thoughts Today …

Read Mark 4:26-29

In this short but powerful parable, told only by Mark, Jesus shows that the same seed that is so vulnerable during the sowing stage (vs. 3-7) has inherent strength during the germinating stage as it grows in a responsive life.

This is the other side of the agricultural picture. The first story in this chapter, the parable of the soils, focuses on how we receive the seed. This parable emphasizes the mysterious life-force in the seed. Notice that the farmer can Plant in suitable soil, Reap when the harvest has come, but he cannot Germinate. This is a decision made by the soil in cooperation with God as it allows the mysterious life-force of the seed to burst forth in growth. Paul uses a similar metaphor for faith growing when he writes:

> *I planted the seed, Apollos watered it, but God made it grow.*
> *So neither he who plants nor he who waters is anything,*
> *but only God, who makes things grow.*
> *1 Corinthians 3:6-7*

Our attempts to force spiritual growth in someone's life make as much sense as digging up seeds to encourage (or threaten) them toward greater or faster growth.

1. Why do we want to quickly see the "results" of our ministry?

2. What can we be doing while we wait?

Jesus describes three periods in the experience of the farmer. They are stages of spiritual growth and, for Jesus' disciples, they are the stages of ministry:

Stage 1 — Faithful Sowing — "A man scatters seed on the ground" (vs. 26) This is not selective or selfish sowing. We cannot prejudge the soil. Our job is to sow the seed, not judge the soil.

3. What are your opportunities to sow God's seed?

Stage 2 — Patient Waiting — "The seed sprouts and grows, though he does not know how" (vs. 27) Patience comes only to the one who knows that the harvest is in the hands of God. In this case, not knowing the future produces patient prayer, not impatient worry.

4. Why is patience difficult for some, but natural for others?

5. What is the difference between patience and apathy?

Stage 3 — Joyful Reaping — "He puts the sickle to it" (vs. 29). Notice the attitude. This is privileged reaping, not prideful reaping. Compare Paul's attitude above (1 Co 3:6-7). He knows that God is the power. And so, our participation is a privilege. There is no room for pride or impatience, only joy and thanksgiving. And remember, sometimes another of God's servants will reap what you have sown (Jn 4:37-38).

6. What happens to faith and ministry when pride replaces humility?

7. What do joy and humility have in common?

Even today this story is acted out every time a farmer plants a seed. It is a story that brings together Faith and Power … the faith of the farmer in the power God put in the seed.

Mark 4:26-29

26 He also said, "This is what the kingdom of God is like. A man scatters seed on the ground. 27 Night and day, whether he sleeps or gets up, the seed sprouts and grows, though he does not know how. 28 All by itself the soil produces grain — first the stalk, then the head, then the full kernel in the head. 29 As soon as the grain is ripe, he puts the sickle to it, because the harvest has come."

My Thoughts Today …

Week 3

What I Learned This Week …

… About Jesus

… About Ministry

… About Myself

Day 22
4:30-34

Day 23
4:35-41

Week 4 *The Wounded*
Day 22-28 *Mark 4:30-6:6*

Day 24
5:1-13

Day 25
5:14-20

Day 26
5:21-34

Day 27
5:35-43

Day 28
6:1-6

The Wounded

Mark 4:30-6:6

This week, as you walk with Jesus, you will see his heart open wide to those around him: the sick, the suffering, and the weak.

As you meet a hated demoniac, a hard-hearted hometown, and a frightened woman, see Jesus' compassion overflow into action. See him enter into the wounded world of those around him, not to watch, but to help.

My Prayer For This Week …

Read Mark 4:30-34

Taking a mustard seed, a Jewish symbol of insignificance, Jesus teaches a powerful lesson of hope and expectancy. It is a lesson needed by both ancient and modern followers. Great results have often come from small beginnings:

· A simple staff — Ex 4:2-5	· Five small stones — 1 Sa 17:40, 49-50
· A small cloud — 1 Ki 18:44-45	· A rejected stone — Ps 118:22
· A tender "shoot" — Isa 11:1-2	· Five loaves and two small fish — Jn 6:9-13

Later, Paul explains why God brings great results from small beginnings:

> *Brothers, think of what you were when you were called.*
> *Not many of you were wise by human standards;*
> *not many were influential; not many were of noble birth.*
> *But God chose the foolish things of the world to shame the wise;*
> *God chose the weak things of the world to shame the strong.*
> *He chose the lowly things of this world and the despised things and the things that are not—*
> *to nullify the things that are, so that no one may boast before him.*
> *1 Corinthians 1:26-29*

1. Why is it powerful for greatness to come from weakness?

Farmers have often wondered how such small seeds can produce such large plants. Jesus takes advantage of his listener's familiarity with the mustard seed. In the preceding parable (vs. 26-29), the message is about the process of growth. But here the lesson is about the potential for growth in a person's life or in a church.

Small Beginnings —"The smallest seed" (vs. 31). Compared to all that is happening in Palestine — the movement of Roman troops, the busy trade routes of merchants and the activity of Jewish pilgrims — Jesus' small band of believers must feel insignificant. The same is true today. We are so preoccupied with national and international stories and events that we often miss God's tiny seeds:

· A mother's prayer	· A boy's imagination	· A teacher's hard work
· A girl's joy	· A man's silent commitment	· A friend's endurance

2. What hope does this parable give you when you feel that your life, your family or your church is insignificant?

Gradual Growth — "When planted, it grows" (vs. 32). Jesus taught them "as much as they could understand." And his work in our lives not only matches our ability to understand but also our openness and willingness to follow.

3. What can you do to become more open to God's work in your life?

Great Results — "Becomes the largest" (vs. 32). The "birds of the air" are Jewish symbols for the Gentiles (Eze 17:23; 31:6; Da 4:11, 12, 21). They picture a kingdom that is planted on Jewish soil, but soon spreads out its branches to a much wider audience.

4. How can God begin growing his kingdom in your life?

5. How wide is your vision of God's kingdom?

Mark 4:30-34

30 Again he said, "What shall we say the kingdom of God is like, or what parable shall we use to describe it? 31 It is like a mustard seed, which is the smallest seed you plant in the ground. 32 Yet when planted, it grows and becomes the largest of all garden plants, with such big branches that the birds of the air can perch in its shade." 33 With many similar parables Jesus spoke the word to them, as much as they could understand. 34 He did not say anything to them without using a parable. But when he was alone with his own disciples, he explained everything.

My Thoughts Today …

Read Mark 4:35-41

The scene now shifts to "the other side" or the east side of the Sea of Galilee. After an exhausting day of teaching and answering questions, the disciples take Jesus aboard their boat and try to put six miles of water behind them.

1. **Why is it important to occasionally "get away" and "find a change of scenery"?**

2. **How do you do this?**

3. **What indicates that this is an impromptu trip?**

But the Sea of Galilee, 680 feet below sea level and deep-set in a basin, surrounded by high mountains, is subject to sudden storms. With the waves washing into the boat, even these seasoned fishermen, who have spent their lives fishing on this huge lake, are afraid. They panic.

4. **When faced with a crisis, our real nature emerges — Why?**

5. **Of the two, which usually emerges during your crisis — faith or fear?**

After being awakened by these frightened disciples, Jesus very calmly gives a word of power to the raging storm — "Quiet! Be still!" His command is instantly obeyed and a dead calm appears as suddenly as the storm had. It brings to mind Psalm 107:23-29.

> *Others went out on the sea in ships …*
> *he spoke and stirred up a tempest that lifted high the waves.*
> *They mounted up to the heavens and went down to the depths;*
> *in their peril their courage melted away.*
> *They reeled and staggered like drunken men; they were at their wits' end.*
> *They cried out to the Lord in their trouble, and he brought them out of their distress.*
> *He stilled the storm to a whisper; the waves of the sea were hushed.*

Jesus' action challenges the narrow political and military view the Twelve have of him. He demonstrates that he shares with God the power of nature itself. This seems to frighten the disciples even more than the storm. It is becoming more and more difficult for them to put Jesus into a tidy little category:

· Carpenter?	· Political Leader?	· Magician?
· Prophet?	· Messiah?	· Rabbi?

Now the question becomes more urgent — "Who is this?" (vs. 41). In other words "He is not who we thought he was." These shaken disciples have seen an awesome power. This demonstration is clearly outside the realm of their simple earthly categories. There are only two possible options open to them — to close their minds or to open them wide enough to take him in.

6. **Why is it difficult to expand our small view of God each time we see more?**

7. **Why do we put off deciding to trust God even when we know that the many crises that touch our lives cannot be avoided?**

8. **Decide in prayer to open yourself to what God will be teaching you.**

35 That day when evening came, he said to his disciples, "Let us go over to the other side." 36 Leaving the crowd behind, they took him along, just as he was, in the boat. There were also other boats with him. 37 A furious squall came up, and the waves broke over the boat, so that it was nearly swamped. 38 Jesus was in the stern, sleeping on a cushion. The disciples woke him and said to him, "Teacher, don't you care if we drown?" 39 He got up, rebuked the wind and said to the waves, "Quiet! Be still!" Then the wind died down and it was completely calm. 40 He said to his disciples, "Why are you so afraid? Do you still have no faith?" 41 They were terrified and asked each other, "Who is this? Even the wind and the waves obey him!"

My Thoughts Today ...

Read Mark 5:1-13

This graphic story pictures an aimless life receiving direction and purpose. The scene is set at the edge of the district of the Decapolis on the southeast side of the Sea of Galilee. Here, Jesus again encounters a life deeply entangled with trouble:

The Man — Notice that the demoniac is living with no purpose:

· He cries out (vs. 5) — He is disoriented, wandering and anguished.

· He lives in the tombs (vs. 3) — This man lives with the dead. Death stalks him. Death always stalks a life with no purpose.

· He is alone — He has no support and no encouragement.

· He cuts himself (vs. 5) — He is sleepless, anguished and suicidal.

· He is out of control (vs. 4) — He is either avoided or captured because he has no center of control, no purpose and no hope.

1.   Have you ever felt like you were out of control or that something evil was in control of you?

2.   What was it? How did God rescue you?

The Legion — Contrary to the Hollywood version, evil must be enfleshed, incarnated. Jesus does not encounter floating apparitions or disembodied spirits because evil is not abstract. It is real. It dwells in real people. It grips human beings.

3.   Why is it so popular today to paint abstract pictures of evil?

4.   Why do many only conceive of evil in dramatic ways?

5.   How can the quieter, more gradual evil be even more deadly?

The Confrontation — This man, who normally avoided people, "ran" to Jesus. This is the first step toward finding a life purpose.

6.   What did he see in Jesus that overcame his fear?

When Jesus asks for a name, those possessing the man give a number. They identify themselves simply as "Legion" a term normally used to refer to a division of the Roman army numbering at least 6,000 men in strength. This man is possessed by a collection of uncoordinated impulses and forces. Having no unity of will, he falls to his knees in frustration, confession and petition. This is the second step toward finding a life purpose.

7.   Is it difficult for you to admit failure or to confess sin? Why?

The Healing — Taking the third step out of his self-destructive world, the man surrenders to the only one who can provide hope, meaning and purpose.

8.   What is the most difficult part of your life to surrender?

The man who had been possessed by fear, loneliness, guilt, meaninglessness and pain is now re-possessed by God. In the presence of Jesus evil is subdued (vs. 6), but only for those who run to him and surrender. Re-possession is found through — Choice, Confession and Commitment.

9.   Describe your own progress in each of these three areas.

Mark 5:1-13

1 They went across the lake to the region of the Gerasenes. 2 When Jesus got out of the boat, a man with an evil spirit came from the tombs to meet him. 3 This man lived in the tombs, and no one could bind him any more, not even with a chain. 4 For he had often been chained hand and foot, but he tore the chains apart and broke the irons on his feet. No one was strong enough to subdue him. 5 Night and day among the tombs and in the hills he would cry out and cut himself with stones. 6 When he saw Jesus from a distance, he ran and fell on his knees in front of him. 7 He shouted at the top of his voice, "What do you want with me, Jesus, Son of the Most High God? Swear to God that you won't torture me!" 8 For Jesus had said to him, "Come out of this man, you evil spirit!" 9 Then Jesus asked him, "What is your name?" "My name is Legion," he replied, "for we are many." 10 And he begged Jesus again and again not to send them out of the area. 11 A large herd of pigs was feeding on the nearby hillside. 12 The demons begged Jesus, "Send us among the pigs; allow us to go into them." 13 He gave them permission, and the evil spirits came out and went into the pigs. The herd, about two thousand in number, rushed down the steep bank into the lake and were drowned.

My Thoughts Today ...

Read Mark 5:14-20

This is the sequel to yesterday's dramatic story — the reaction of those watching.

The Neighbors — It might seem that those living in the region would be delighted to find a man who had been violent and uncontrollable now "sitting … dressed and in his right mind" (vs. 15). After all, this is the man who had been wandering, naked and totally out of control! But, instead of joy and relief "they were afraid and they begged Jesus to leave their region." No questions or curiosity. No joy in the man's good fortune. They just want Jesus to leave. They no longer have a scapegoat — a mad man to blame all their failures and frustrations on. Notice once again, the choice — faith or fear?

1. Why were they afraid? Why did they want him to leave?

2. When something is obviously good, but you don't fully understand it, do you ask and investigate, or do you avoid the whole thing?

The Disciples — Most of the time this story is read as an encounter that Jesus had. It is easy to forget that his constant companions, the twelve disciples, were in the boat with him when it landed, and saw the whole episode.

3. Imagine how they would have felt seeing this screaming maniac running toward them.

4. We don't know if they even got out of the boat — Would you?

They had observed healing and exorcism before. But this time, instead of joy and celebration, they see a reaction of fear (vs. 15) and resentment (vs. 17).

5. Is it hard for you to serve others when your service is criticized? Why?

The Man Himself — The ex-maniac wants to join Jesus and his disciples, but Jesus has another mission for him. So, with Jesus' encouragement, the man returns home to tell his family and friends what has happened. Perhaps it is the geographical difference that allows Jesus to command that this story be told (5:19), while back on Jewish soil "the messianic secret" continues (1:25, 34, 44; 3:12; 5:43; 7:24, 36; 8:26, 30; 9:9, 30).

6. What motivated the healed demoniac to share his story?

7. Do you have family or friends who have never heard your story?

8. How could you tell them?

9. How would they react?

10. Don't forget to leave room for God to work.

There is an important footnote to this story. Later Jesus will come back to the Decapolis area and will find that, probably through the influence of this thankful man, the people have become more receptive (7:31-8:9). The lesson? Even though our help might be criticized or even refused, the seed is planted. As Jesus said, the sower does "the hard work" (Jn 4:37-38).

11. Why is "sowing" or "serving" the "hard work"?

Mark 5:14-20

14 Those tending the pigs ran off and reported this in the town and countryside, and the people went out to see what had happened. 15 When they came to Jesus, they saw the man who had been possessed by the legion of demons, sitting there, dressed and in his right mind; and they were afraid. 16 Those who had seen it told the people what had happened to the demon-possessed man — and told about the pigs as well. 17 Then the people began to plead with Jesus to leave their region. 18 As Jesus was getting into the boat, the man who had been demon-possessed begged to go with him. 19 Jesus did not let him, but said, "Go home to your family and tell them how much the Lord has done for you, and how he has had mercy on you." 20 So the man went away and began to tell in the Decapolis how much Jesus had done for him. And all the people were amazed.

My Thoughts Today …

Read Mark 5:21-34

After finding no rest Jesus returns to the west side of the sea only to be met by a huge crowd. From this mass of people emerges two intertwined stories. Although they picture totally different ends of the social spectrum, they show that in their moment of need, the well-known ruler and the unknown woman are equals.

1. How does "human need" seem to break down all social barriers?

2. How wide is your scope of service to people?

As Jesus lands he is immediately met by one of the synagogue notables, Jairus. It is an interruption, but an interruption of faith. Jairus is desperate, searching for help.

3. Interruptions — how do you usually handle them?

Jairus is not the only desperate person in this story. There is a woman whose suffering is as old as Jairus' daughter (12 years). She is poor, weak, friendless and unknown. In her pain she thinks, "If I just touch his clothes" (vs. 28). So, she interrupts Jairus' interruption.

4. How would you feel if, like Jairus, your request for help was interrupted?

5. What does this tell you about Jairus?

The desperate woman only wants to slip up behind Jesus to steal a miracle, but Jesus feels her anguish and insists on personal contact. She "trembles with fear" because she, an unclean woman, has touched a Rabbi and made him unclean (Lev 15:19ff). But notice Jesus' reaction: He calmly calls her "daughter" – the only time he addresses a woman so. He confirms her cure, putting her years-old fear and anguish to rest. He then compliments her "faith."

6. Why is Jesus so gentle with her?

There are two powerful lessons to be learned from this encounter:

Beginning Faith — The woman begins in superstition. She sees Jesus' power as magical and mechanical. She feels no need to personally know him or for him to know her. She has no plan to ask for help or even to express gratitude. Her faith is immature. But Jesus doesn't wait until her understanding or her approach is fully correct before he acts. He looks deeper. He looks at her heart.

7. What did God require of you when your faith began in immaturity?

8. What do you require of others? Is there a difference?

Growing Faith — Jesus allows an immature start, but he immediately begins to perfect her faith. She cannot remain anonymous. He wants to be her friend not just her healer. But he also wants to move her faith from concealed to revealed. Revealed not only to her but also to her community.

9. Is your faith more Concealed or Revealed? Why?

We are so easily irritated. Crowds irritate us. Interruptions irritate us more. How much we need to see Jesus responding to needs — personally, individually and patiently.

10. Our culture thrives on consolidation, assembly lines, form letters. How has this affected and damaged ministry? How can we regain the "personal" touch of Jesus?

Mark 5:21-34

21 When Jesus had again crossed over by boat to the other side of the lake, a large crowd gathered around him while he was by the lake. 22 Then one of the synagogue rulers, named Jairus, came there. Seeing Jesus, he fell at his feet 23 and pleaded earnestly with him, "My little daughter is dying. Please come and put your hands on her so that she will be healed and live." 24 So Jesus went with him. A large crowd followed and pressed around him. 25 And a woman was there who had been subject to bleeding for twelve years. 26 She had suffered a great deal under the care of many doctors and had spent all she had, yet instead of getting better she grew worse. 27 When she heard about Jesus, she came up behind him in the crowd and touched his cloak, 28 because she thought, "If I just touch his clothes, I will be healed." 29 Immediately her bleeding stopped and she felt in her body that she was freed from her suffering. 30 At once Jesus realized that power had gone out from him. He turned around in the crowd and asked, "Who touched my clothes?" 31 "You see the people crowding against you," his disciples answered, "and yet you can ask, 'Who touched me?'" 32 But Jesus kept looking around to see who had done it. 33 Then the woman, knowing what had happened to her, came and fell at his feet and, trembling with fear, told him the whole truth. 34 He said to her, "Daughter, your faith has healed you. Go in peace and be freed from your suffering."

My Thoughts Today ...

Read Mark 5:35-43

Mark likes to sandwich one story in between the layers of another story. Yesterday's story of the suffering woman is sandwiched in between two layers of the story of Jairus and his daughter. Today the story continues with Jairus waiting.

1. **Put yourself in Jairus' place. What are you feeling as Jesus talks to this interrupting woman?**

2. **How do you feel when you hear the message that your daughter has died?**

It was probably not easy for Jairus to come to Jesus for help in the first place. Jesus has already made many religious and political enemies (cf. 3:6) and approaching him in public will be risky. This is why both Nicodemus and Joseph of Arimathea are "secret" disciples (see Jn 3:1-2; 19:38-39). But Jairus is desperate. He is fully aware of how great his need is. And so, he openly comes to Jesus in the light of day.

3. **How do pain and tragedy humble pride and soften hearts?**

Jairus has been waiting. But sadly, a group of men come with the message he has been dreading. He doesn't have to wait any longer.

Faith or Fear? — The message is "Your daughter is dead" (vs. 35), but Jesus ignores this conclusion and again draws the contrast between faith and fear. On one end of the social spectrum, the suffering woman had to choose between faith and fear. Now, on the other end, Jairus has to choose.

4. **How do you usually analyze the future ... with faith or fear?**

5. **How does this story move you toward faith?**

Crying or Laughing? — Professional mourners were a common sight in the ancient east, especially in connection with someone as important as a synagogue ruler. But Jesus puts them all out of Jairus' house! Only real mourners are allowed. Only they will be comforted. Only they need it. Unbelief laughs at God's promise. Faith trusts in it.

6. **Why did Jesus put out those who laughed? Why didn't he allow them to see this miracle?**

Dead or Asleep? — "Sleep" as a euphemism for death was common among the ancients. But Jesus speaks in a radically different sense — much like the early Christians. They described the dead as "sleeping" (1 Co 11:30; 15:6; 1 Th 4:13-15) because they believed the dead would one day be awakened.

7. **Imagine that day — your daughter is raised! How would you feel? What would you say and do?**

Talitha Koum! — With words that her mother used every morning to wake her, Jesus raises the little girl to her feet and rekindles her life. His humanity is apparent as he so easily moves from Supernatural – "Don't be afraid, just believe" – to Natural – "Give her something to eat" (vs. 43). His service is offered with no strings. His healing comes from compassion, not a desire for personal prestige — "He gave strict orders not to let anyone know about this" (vs. 43).

8. **How can I know that my service is motivated purely?**

9. **Ask God to help you see the joy of service with no strings.**

35 While Jesus was still speaking, some men came from the house of Jairus, the synagogue ruler. "Your daughter is dead," they said. "Why bother the teacher any more?" 36 Ignoring what they said, Jesus told the synagogue ruler, "Don't be afraid; just believe." 37 He did not let anyone follow him except Peter, James and John the brother of James. 38 When they came to the home of the synagogue ruler, Jesus saw a commotion, with people crying and wailing loudly. 39 He went in and said to them, "Why all this commotion and wailing? The child is not dead but asleep." 40 But they laughed at him. After he put them all out, he took the child's father and mother and the disciples who were with him, and went in where the child was. 41 He took her by the hand and said to her, "Talitha koum!" (which means, "Little girl, I say to you, get up!"). 42 Immediately the girl stood up and walked around (she was twelve years old). At this they were completely astonished. 43 He gave strict orders not to let anyone know about this, and told them to give her something to eat.

My Thoughts Today …

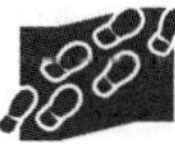

Read Mark 6:1-6 (cf. Luke 4:16-30)

Jesus now leaves Capernaum to preach in Galilee. He begins 25 miles away in his "hometown" Nazareth (Lk 4:16). The reaction to him is amazing. Back in Capernaum he had stilled a sea, healed a woman and raised a child from the dead. Yet here, in his hometown, he is opposed. The term Mark uses to describe the reaction is eskandalizonto (vs. 3), from which we get our word "scandal." Jesus is a scandal. His own people are jealous. It is as though they are asking, "Who does he think he is? He's no better than us." Whether we call it familiarity, prejudice or preconceived judgment, it can distort our view and even has the power to completely blind us to reality.

1. Why is it sometimes hard for friends and family to accept growth and change in us?

Probably the rumor is still circulating that Jesus is illegitimate. This could be the meaning of "Mary's son" (vs. 3). To identify a man by his mother is a calculated insult suggesting that he was born to an unmarried woman.

2. Describe the difference between the "Who do you think you are" attitude and the "My, how you've grown" attitude.

The whole town opposes Jesus. But at the same time, there is an undeniable depth and truth in his words. This puzzles those who have watched him grow up. Rather than accept his truth and admit his wisdom, they are full of questions:

> *Where did this man get these things?*
> *Isn't this Mary's son …?*
> *Isn't this the carpenter?*
> *Aren't his sisters here with us?*
> *What's this wisdom that has been given him?*

The internal conflict storms. On the one hand, they know him. But on the other hand, he is amazing beyond recognition. His truth is hard to accept.

3. How does doubt affect faith? What prevents you from accepting something you know is true?

4. It is difficult for you to admit and accept progress and growth in someone you have known since their childhood? Why?

One of the most candid statements in the gospels is "He could not do any miracles there, except …" (vs. 5). This clearly underlines the importance of faith and also distinguishes Jesus' healing stories from simple magic. Jesus' healings are not haphazard demonstrations by a sorcerer or magician. They are always tied to a personal faith that cooperates and surrenders to the will of God. It seems that, here in Jesus' hometown, the "stumbling block" is not a failure to believe that Jesus can do these things (vs. 2), but a sheer jealously, an antagonism and a refusal to cooperate.

5. Describe the best way to cooperate with Jesus.

Once Jesus marveled at the great faith of a Gentile centurion (Lk 7:9). Here he marvels at the great "lack of faith" in his own hometown (vs. 6).

6. How would Jesus describe your faith?

1 Jesus left there and went to his hometown, accompanied by his disciples. 2 When the Sabbath came, he began to teach in the synagogue, and many who heard him were amazed. "Where did this man get these things?" they asked. "What's this wisdom that has been given him, that he even does miracles! 3 Isn't this the carpenter? Isn't this Mary's son and the brother of James, Joseph, Judas and Simon? Aren't his sisters here with us?" And they took offense at him. 4 Jesus said to them, "Only in his hometown, among his relatives and in his own house is a prophet without honor." 5 He could not do any miracles there, except lay his hands on a few sick people and heal them. 6 And he was amazed at their lack of faith. Then Jesus went around teaching from village to village.

My Thoughts Today …

Week 4
What I Learned This Week ...

... About Jesus

... About Ministry

... About Myself

Day 29
6:7-13

Day 30
6:14-29

Week 5   The People
Day 29-35   Mark 6:7-7:23

Day 31
6:30-46

Day 32
6:47-52

Day 33
6:53-56

Day 34
7:1-13

Day 35
7:14-23

The People

Mark 6:7-7:23

This week, as you walk with Jesus, you will be impressed by the wide variety of people in his story. You will meet a corrupt king, a cruel queen, large crowds, lonely individuals, unfriendly towns, and rigid religionists. You will find that Jesus' story includes them all.

Your story is also filled with people. Try to bring his style into your week of people.

My Prayer For This Week …

Read Mark 6:7-13

Jesus knows that eventually, he will entrust his mission to the Twelve. So he begins now to give them more responsibility with some "hands on" training. Even though the details of his instructions to the Twelve reflect the first century, behind this story are timeless principles which speak to ministry today:

"Two by Two" — No doubt Jesus sends them in pairs because of the scriptural and common-sense truth that "two are better than one" (Ecc 4:9). Everyone can benefit from the power of combined wisdom, counsel, insight and encouragement.

1.   **Do you believe this?**

2.   **Are you a loner?**

3.   **How is ministry strengthened by strong Christian relationships?**

"Take Nothing For The Journey" — These special instructions are not intended to bring poverty or hardship. Instead, they simply show the urgency and the importance of the mission. They need to travel light. They should not delay with extensive preparation, or needless equipment.

4.   **How can our possessions become a hindrance to our ministry?**

5.   **Is your life "simple" enough so that you can relate to all kinds of people in ministry?**

6.   **What needs to change in your life?**

"No Bread, No Bag" — The "bag" mentioned here is a religious "collection bag." This was standard equipment for the wandering preachers of the time who travel from village to village collecting contributions for their temple or god. Jesus seems to be saying, "Do not be greedy. You are on a mission of giving, not getting."

7.   **What turns a ministry from being other-centered to self-centered?**

8.   **How can you prevent this in your life?**

"Enter a House" — Unlike the fenced privacy of our own culture, in the ancient world, hospitality was a sacred duty. When travelers entered a village, hospitality was customarily offered to them. Jesus is telling his disciples that if doors and hearts are shut, take God's message elsewhere. The factor determining how long they stay is the response given to their message. Do the people "welcome" and "listen" (vs. 11)?

9.   **How hard is it for you to "enter" into a person's life (cf. I Th 2:8)?**

10. **What would be your first step into a life that is open to God?**

"Shake The Dust Off" — The Mishnah (Berakoth 9.5) prohibits a man from entering the Jerusalem temple "with dust on his feet" because the temple was holy. Here, the disciples are to rid themselves of the dust of an unresponsive town because their mission is as sacred as worship.

11. **When a Christian begins to ignore the mission of God, what begins to happen to their worship of God? (cf. Ro 12:1-2)**

12. **How can you tell if someone "welcomes" the God that lives in you?**

7 Calling the Twelve to him, he sent them out two by two and gave them authority over evil spirits. 8 These were his instructions: "Take nothing for the journey except a staff — no bread, no bag, no money in your belts. 9 Wear sandals but not an extra tunic. 10 Whenever you enter a house, stay there until you leave that town. 11 And if any place will not welcome you or listen to you, shake the dust off your feet when you leave, as a testimony against them." 12 They went out and preached that people should repent. 13 They drove out many demons and anointed many sick people with oil and healed them.

My Thoughts Today ...

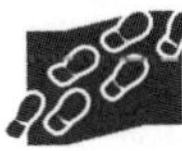

Read Mark 6:14-29

This is a story of hostility, bitterness and conscience. It brings to an end the story of a prophet who boldly steps into the tangle of hostility, jealously and fear. After mentioning John the Baptist's imprisonment (1:14), now, in "flashback" form, the story centers on his death. Palestine is divided into four regions, each ruled by a Tetrarch. Herod Antipas controls Galilee. And though he comes from a family of political rulers, this family also has a history of matrimonial entanglements that defy description:

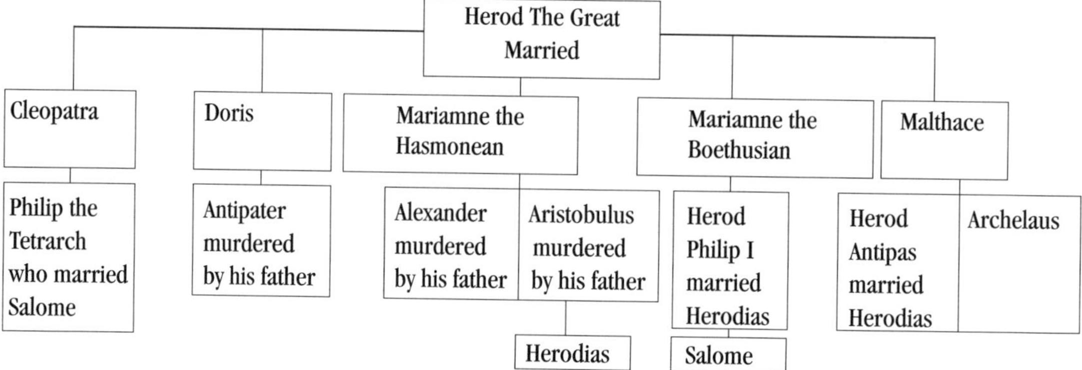

Because of John's preaching, Herod has him killed at the fortress of Machaerus by the Dead Sea. And now, because of the mission of the disciples (vs. 7-13), Herod begins to hear about Jesus. This frightens him because the common speculation is that Jesus is a great leader from the past — perhaps the recent past. Herod has cut off the head of one witness, but he cannot silence God's inner witness, his own conscience:

Competing Emotions — "Feared ... protected ... liked to listen" (vs. 20) — Herod is indecisive, unsure and hesitating. He both respects and hates John. He respects his honesty and is threatened by his courage.

1. Why is it dangerous to keep hearing God's message, knowing it is true, and yet never do anything to change?

Competing Convictions — "Distressed, but ... his oaths ... his guests" (vs. 26) — A rash promise from a drunk king sets up a forced decision — to be embarrassed or to murder. His indecisive life is easily pushed into a forced choice. The only choice humans cannot make is the choice to not choose.

2. Think of a time when you did something wrong to please others.

3. What could help you resist this pressure?

Competing Loyalties — "Herodias nursed a grudge" (vs. 19) — Her hatred and callousness brings ruin to everyone. She not only wants to control John, but everyone else as well. And so she brings disaster to her husband, her daughter and probably all her relationships.

4. Describe the kind of life that wants to control others.

5. Herodias had a grudge. Where do grudges lead?

14 King Herod heard about this, for Jesus' name had become well known. Some were saying, "John the Baptist has been raised from the dead, and that is why miraculous powers are at work in him." 15 Others said, "He is Elijah." And still others claimed, "He is a prophet, like one of the prophets of long ago." 16 But when Herod heard this, he said, "John, the man I beheaded, has been raised from the dead!" 17 For Herod himself had given orders to have John arrested, and he had him bound and put in prison. He did this because of Herodias, his brother Philip's wife, whom he had married. 18 For John had been saying to Herod, "It is not lawful for you to have your brother's wife." 19 So Herodias nursed a grudge against John and wanted to kill him. But she was not able to, 20 because Herod feared John and protected him, knowing him to be a righteous and holy man. When Herod heard John, he was greatly puzzled; yet he liked to listen to him. 21 Finally the opportune time came. On his birthday Herod gave a banquet for his high officials and military commanders and the leading men of Galilee. 22 When the daughter of Herodias came in and danced, she pleased Herod and his dinner guests. The king said to the girl, "Ask me for anything you want, and I'll give it to you." 23 And he promised her with an oath, "Whatever you ask I will give you, up to half my kingdom." 24 She went out and said to her mother, "What shall I ask for?" "The head of John the Baptist," she answered. 25 At once the girl hurried in to the king with the request: "I want you to give me right now the head of John the Baptist on a platter." 26 The king was greatly distressed, but because of his oaths and his dinner guests, he did not want to refuse her. 27 So he immediately sent an executioner with orders to bring John's head. The man went, beheaded John in the prison, 28 and brought back his head on a platter. He presented it to the girl, and she gave it to her mother. 29 On hearing of this, John's disciples came and took his body and laid it in a tomb.

My Thoughts Today ...

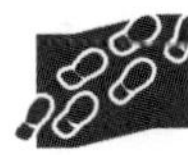

Read Mark 6:30-46

This is the only miracle recorded by all of the gospel writers. It is usually read as an example of Jesus' lordship over nature. However, there is a deeper issue at stake. Mark hints that a conflict, existing between Jesus and the Twelve, surfaces at the gathering of the 5,000 men (6:52; 8:17-21):

"Reported … All They Had Done" (vs. 30) — The Twelve return from their mission (6:7), and though Jesus has instructed them to preach repentance and to heal, is this all that they have done? What about this huge crowd (vs. 31)? Where have they come from? What brings them together? John, in his telling of the story, says that the crowd has come to make Jesus king "by force" (Jn 6:15). In other words, this is not a simple picnic in the park, but a widespread and concerted political movement.

1.   Who stirred up the nationalistic hopes of this crowd?

2.   What does the crowd want from Jesus?

"Sheep Without A Shepherd" (vs. 34) — When Jesus perceives the purpose of the crowd, immediately the phrase "sheep without a shepherd" comes to his mind. The Old Testament consistently uses this description to picture the nation of Israel without a political leader (Nu 27:17; I Ki 22:17; 2 Ch 18:16; Ps 78:70-72; Isa 44:28; 63:11; Eze 34:1-5; Zec 10:2; 11:4-12). According to Numbers 27, Moses prayed that God would raise up a man to lead the nation of Israel "so the Lord's people will not be like a sheep without a shepherd" (vs. 17). Like the feeding of the 5,000, this Old Testament incident also took place in the wilderness and the man chosen was "Joshua," the Hebrew equivalent for "Jesus."

Jesus does see himself as a shepherd (Jn 10:11), but his style of leadership clashes with the political and military hopes of both the Twelve and the 5,000 men they have gathered.

3.   What emotion probably fills Jesus upon seeing the 5,000?

"He Began Teaching" (vs. 34) — Jesus knows that he is not a military leader like Joshua. His mission is vastly different. So, with his trademark teaching style, he begins to disarm the army.

4.   Speculate — what did Jesus teach to the 5,000?

"Made His Disciples Get In The Boat" (vs. 45) — This is not a chance crowd, but a nationalistic rebellion. Many people have come with high hopes and explosive potential. So Jesus takes extra firm steps to stop the army from forming. Both Matthew and Mark literally say that Jesus "forced" the Twelve to leave.

5.   Why is Jesus upset with the Twelve?

6.   Why does he want them to leave?

"He Went Up On A Mountainside" (vs. 46) — Jesus is clearly a man of prayer. But among the many times that Matthew, Luke and John show him praying, Mark focuses on three occasions. This is the second time Mark highlights Jesus praying and like the other two (1:35; 14:32-42), this is a time of crisis.

7.   What is Jesus most likely praying about?

8.   What do you do in time of crisis?

30 The apostles gathered around Jesus and reported to him all they had done and taught. 31 Then, because so many people were coming and going that they did not even have a chance to eat, he said to them, "Come with me by yourselves to a quiet place and get some rest." 32 So they went away by themselves in a boat to a solitary place. 33 But many who saw them leaving recognized them and ran on foot from all the towns and got there ahead of them. 34 When Jesus landed and saw a large crowd, he had compassion on them, because they were like sheep without a shepherd. So he began teaching them many things. 35 By this time it was late in the day, so his disciples came to him. "This is a remote place," they said, "and it's already very late. 36 Send the people away so they can go to the surrounding countryside and villages and buy themselves something to eat." 37 But he answered, "You give them something to eat." They said to him, "That would take eight months of a man's wages! Are we to go and spend that much on bread and give it to them to eat?" 38 "How many loaves do you have?" he asked. "Go and see." When they found out, they said, "Five — and two fish." 39 Then Jesus directed them to have all the people sit down in groups on the green grass. 40 So they sat down in groups of hundreds and fifties. 41 Taking the five loaves and the two fish and looking up to heaven, he gave thanks and broke the loaves. Then he gave them to his disciples to set before the people. He also divided the two fish among them all. 42 They all ate and were satisfied, 43 and the disciples picked up twelve basketfuls of broken pieces of bread and fish. 44 The number of the men who had eaten was five thousand. 45 Immediately Jesus made his disciples get into the boat and go on ahead of him to Bethsaida, while he dismissed the crowd. 46 After leaving them, he went up on a mountainside to pray.

My Thoughts Today …

Read Mark 6:47-52

Even though it has been eight hours since Jesus sent the Twelve away by boat, they still haven't made four miles. With the wind blowing from the northwest the disciples try to row to Bethsaida (vs. 45). But they again find themselves fighting a Galilean storm that will take them, not to Bethsaida, but to Gennesaret (vs. 53). Jesus sees their predicament from the mountain where he has been praying (vs. 46). And after sending them away in failure, he now returns with the next lesson.

1. **How can Jesus return to such closed and stubborn disciples?**

2. **Who in your life "tries" your patience?**

3. **How can you apply Jesus' attitude to the relationships that frustrate you the most?**

This is the third picture of misunderstanding in chapter six. The first is Jesus' hometown (vs. 1-6). The second is Herod (vs. 14-16). And now (vs. 52), it is the disciples. It is clear that they still do not understand the real power of Jesus. And this is in spite of the incredible things they have seen and heard:

They have seen his compassion for the outcast, the poor and the sick.

They have witnessed his refusal to be another warlord like Joshua or David.

They have listened to his teachings on the real nature of the kingdom.

They have been given power to share in his mission.

But what they have seen and heard has still not unseated their own entrenched view of Jesus, the kingdom and their own future. Their minds are "closed" (vs. 52), as they stubbornly hang on to their political hopes. They still see Jesus as a religious opportunist, collecting his following to lead a crusade of political liberation.

Amazingly Jesus remains true to his disciples though he "could have passed them by" as Moffatt translates verse 48. Instead, with compassion, ("don't be afraid"), he first rescues, then stays with them, in spite of their stubbornness. Consider three hard facts:

Hard Sea — After seeing their plight Jesus comes to the disciples, "walking on the lake." In the Old Testament this was a sign of divine presence. The sea was often used to symbolize unrestrained chaos, and God's power over this anarchy was also often pictured as a simple walk upon the waters (Job 9:8; Ps 77:19; Isa 43:16; Hab 3:15).

Solid Lord — As soon as the disciples see Jesus on the water, their fear and insecurity again take over. But just as quickly, Jesus calls out to them, and the phrase he uses to identify himself literally means "I AM" — the well-known Old Testament name for God (Isa 43:25; 48:12; 51:12; cf. also Isa 51:9-16).

4. **How did you respond to the last time the Lord amazed you?**

Stubborn Hearts — Jesus' miracles, like his parables contain a message. Therefore they become either the next step forward into a deeper faith for those with "ears to hear" or a step backwards into a stubborn heart.

5. **What were the disciples missing that they should have understood?**

6. **How does stubbornness "close" a heart?**

7. **How do you usually respond to a stubborn person? How does Jesus?**

47 When evening came, the boat was in the middle of the lake, and he was alone on land. 48 He saw the disciples straining at the oars, because the wind was against them. About the fourth watch of the night he went out to them, walking on the lake. He was about to pass by them, 49 but when they saw him walking on the lake, they thought he was a ghost. They cried out, 50 because they all saw him and were terrified. Immediately he spoke to them and said, "Take courage! It is I. Don't be afraid." 51 Then he climbed into the boat with them, and the wind died down. They were completely amazed, 52 for they had not understood about the loaves; their hearts were hardened.

My Thoughts Today …

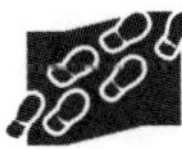

Read Mark 6:53-56

The boat touches land south of Capernaum at Gennesaret, a thickly populated plain, three miles long and over a mile wide. Josephus reports (Jewish War 3.516-521) that it is a fertile plain producing walnuts, palms, figs, olives and grapes.

In spite of the recent disappointments with the Twelve, Jesus is again drawn by human need as the word is spread and the crowds begin to gather around him (vs. 55-56). His mission, although difficult, does not stop!

1. How does Jesus continue after such disappointments?

2. What kind of disappointments are most likely to hinder your ministry?

"People Recognized Jesus" — Everyone knows Jesus. But what is it that they know about him? By this time he is widely know as the Healer. There have been several extraordinary healings:

> · 1:23-31 — A man possessed by an evil spirit
>
> · 1:32-34 — The mass healings from the "whole town"
>
> · 1:40-45 — A man with Leprosy
>
> · 2:1-12 — A paralytic
>
> · 3:1-5 — A man with a shriveled hand
>
> · 3:7-12 — The mass healings of the diseased and demon possessed
>
> · 5:1-20 — The legion of demons
>
> · 5:21-34 — A bleeding woman
>
> · 5:35-43 — The dead daughter of Jairus, a synagogue ruler

"Carried the Sick … Placed the Sick" — As soon as Jesus lands at the shore, he is surrounded by crowds — and everyone comes to get. They come needing and Jesus gives them what they need, but still they come to get. The question is how many will learn to give?

3. List what you came to "get" and what you "got" from God.

4. What grows inside a Christian who only "gets" but never "gives"?

"In the Marketplaces" — It is interesting that everyone knows that Jesus will be in the "marketplaces." He has a reputation for being where the people are. In fact, everywhere he goes, he searches for ways to be among people. It is his way of accomplishing his mission of serving others (10:45).

5. Where does the "average church" carry out its mission today?

6. Where should it carry out its mission?

7. What should change?

Jesus' compassion overrules all of the arguments against ministering to thankless crowds, hardened disciples, and the selfish sick. He never says "You don't deserve my help."

8. What would his ministry of compassion change in your life?

9. What would it change in your family?

10. What would it change in your church?

Mark 6:53-56

53 When they had crossed over, they landed at Gennesaret and anchored there. 54 As soon as they got out of the boat, people recognized Jesus. 55 They ran throughout that whole region and carried the sick on mats to wherever they heard he was. 56 And wherever he went — into villages, towns or countryside — they placed the sick in the marketplaces. They begged him to let them touch even the edge of his cloak, and all who touched him were healed.

My Thoughts Today ...

Read Mark 7:1-13

So far, Jesus has encountered crowds, popularity and activity. On occasion it has brought friction and isolated clashes. But now there begins a whole season of conflict.

Since the Pharisees and Scribes have traveled 65-70 miles up from Jerusalem to find fault with Jesus, it doesn't really matter what the fault is. So, when they see his disciples eating with unwashed hands, they react. But they are concerned with ceremony, not hygiene. And, as usual, Jesus gets to the heart of the matter:

Mutual Discouragement — The Scribes and Pharisees are dissatisfied with Jesus, but the feeling is mutual. He is discouraged with them. Of all people, these religious leaders should be able to recognize his claims and respond to his call. But they can't see. Religious pride has grown so large that it will not recognize God incarnate.

1.   How can pride blind even those who have knowledge — those who should see and recognize?

Devotion To Tradition — The contrast Jesus draws is between the tradition of men and the command of God. Tradition can either support the command of God or it can completely "set aside" the will of God. A religious perspective whose motto is "that's how I was brought up" must not be allowed to overrule what God will continue to teach us. Religious tradition must always be measured by the command of God.

2.   Read through verses 1-12 again and circle the words "tradition" and "command."

3.   If you traced your beliefs back to their source, which of them would originate in command and which of them would originate in tradition?

Hardening Of The Categories — Consider the slow process that eventually places tradition over God's command. It begins with Personal Opinion, which through constant use becomes Established Custom, which through constant use becomes Sacred Tradition, which through constant use becomes Infallible Decree. It is a slow but steady hardening of the categories.

4.   Think of some current examples of Hardening of the Categories.

The Case Of "Corban" — Although the command of God says "honor your father and mother" (Ex 20:12), the tradition of men responds with "Corban" — a Jewish term showing something is "dedicated to God." Selfish children were using this legal fiction to declare their assets "Corban," thereby evading the command of God with a religious loophole. It was a clever disobedience.

5.   What does such "Corban" thinking do to the people around us today?

6.   How can we "nullify" God's word today (vs. 13)?

Worship Or Words — Tradition can build an elaborate lip-service without ever reaching the heart. And so, using Isaiah 29:13, Jesus contrasts ceremony with reality, form with fact. He shows that external religion is worse than useless unless it springs from the inside — from a heart that is open to God.

7.   Describe the essential differences between a religion of the lips and a religion of the heart?

8.   Which is stronger in your own personal faith — lips or heart?

Mark 7:1-13

1 The Pharisees and some of the teachers of the law who had come from Jerusalem gathered around Jesus and 2 saw some of his disciples eating food with hands that were "unclean," that is, unwashed. 3 (The Pharisees and all the Jews do not eat unless they give their hands a ceremonial washing, holding to the tradition of the elders. 4 When they come from the marketplace they do not eat unless they wash. And they observe many other traditions, such as the washing of cups, pitchers and kettles.) 5 So the Pharisees and teachers of the law asked Jesus, "Why don't your disciples live according to the tradition of the elders instead of eating their food with 'unclean' hands?" 6 He replied, "Isaiah was right when he prophesied about you hypocrites; as it is written: "'These people honor me with their lips, but their hearts are far from me. 7 They worship me in vain; their teachings are but rules taught by men.' 8 You have let go of the commands of God and are holding on to the traditions of men." 9 And he said to them: "You have a fine way of setting aside the commands of God in order to observe your own traditions! 10 For Moses said, 'Honor your father and your mother,' and, 'Anyone who curses his father or mother must be put to death.' 11 But you say that if a man says to his father or mother: 'Whatever help you might otherwise have received from me is Corban' (that is, a gift devoted to God), 12 then you no longer let him do anything for his father or mother. 13 Thus you nullify the word of God by your tradition that you have handed down. And you do many things like that."

My Thoughts Today ...

Read Mark 7:14-23

True to form, Jesus turns from the Scribes to the crowd. He wants to tell them where real purity lies. The Pharisees have been focusing on cleaning up the outside. But Jesus says that the real impurity occurs inside — the sins of the "heart" (cf. Mt 23:25-28).

Things or People? — Jesus is moving those who have been following him even further away from a ritual-centered religion. Earlier he had said that people are more important than things — "The Sabbath was made for man, not man for the Sabbath" (2:27). In a similar way he now says that things cannot be religiously clean or unclean, but people can. And furthermore, people cannot be defiled by things, but only by themselves.

1.   Why is damage from the inside the worst kind of damage?

Eating or Thinking? — The only real defilement is what happens to our soul, the only permanent part of us. The soul is the only part that remains after death. And so, a person cannot be polluted by eating, but only by thinking and doing. In fact, there is nothing more potent for good or for evil in a person's character than his imagination — what he allows to live in his private thoughts.

Stomach or Heart? — Food is taken into the stomach, but sin comes out of the heart. The food we eat is digested and the waste is eliminated, but sin remains in the heart and continues to grow, reproduce and bring corruption and death.

2.   Be honest with yourself — what lives in your thoughts that should be rooted out?

Finally, Jesus turns from the crowds to his disciples. Like everyone else, they had been living under the strict Jewish dietary code that categorized all foods as either "clean" or "unclean." In fact, Luke suggests that Peter kept a kosher household for several years after the church had been established (Ac 10:14).

3.   Why does Jesus give the Twelve a more specific and direct teaching?

4.   Why does he call them "dull" (vs. 18)?

If our convictions do not spring from the mind of God, then terrible things will begin to grow inside. Tradition has no real power against evil on the inside (cf. Col 2:23). Following the introductory description of the place where evil resides and multiplies, "evil thoughts," Jesus lists twelve forms of evil that come "out of men's hearts" (Vs 21):

The First Six are plural indicating repeated action ...

Sexual Immorality	Murder	Greed
Theft	Adultery	Malice

The Last Six are singular and describe internal drives ...

Deceit	Envy	Arrogance
Lewdness	Slander	Folly

5.   Why is it true that what lives in the heart will eventually show in our lives?

6.   Be honest with the list in verses 21-23. What is growing inside of you now?

14 Again Jesus called the crowd to him and said, "Listen to me, everyone, and understand this. 15 Nothing outside a man can make him 'unclean' by going into him. Rather, it is what comes out of a man that makes him 'unclean.'" 17 After he had left the crowd and entered the house, his disciples asked him about this parable. 18 "Are you so dull?" he asked. "Don't you see that nothing that enters a man from the outside can make him 'unclean'? 19 For it doesn't go into his heart but into his stomach, and then out of his body." (In saying this, Jesus declared all foods "clean.") 20 He went on: "What comes out of a man is what makes him 'unclean.' 21 For from within, out of men's hearts, come evil thoughts, sexual immorality, theft, murder, adultery, 22 greed, malice, deceit, lewdness, envy, slander, arrogance and folly. 23 All these evils come from inside and make a man 'unclean.'"

My Thoughts Today …

What I Learned This Week ...

... About Jesus

... About Ministry

... About Myself

Day 36
7:24-30

Day 37
7:31-37

Day 38
8:1-10

Day 39
8:11-21

Day 40
8:22-26

Day 41
8:27-30

Day 42
8:31-38

Week 6   The Ministry
Day 36-42   Mark 7:24-8:38

The Ministry

Mark 7:24-8:38

This week, as you walk with Jesus, you will see him fully involved in ministry. Watch him cross racial barriers to give food and healing. Watch faithful friends go to unusual lengths to bring a someone to Jesus. Listen to Jesus explain the ministry of his own death to a stunned group of disciples.

Try to personally answer his question: "What would you give in exchange for your soul?"

My Prayer For This Week …

Read Mark 7:24-30

After the former conflict (7:1-23), Jesus withdraws to the Syrian coast far to the north. Only once before has he left his own land (5:1ff). But this is a major turning point. And so, from the time he enters Gentile territory until he turns toward Jerusalem and his own cross, he will stay on the fringe, seeking seclusion (vs. 24), becoming an exile, a refugee. Jesus is anticipating his death and therefore he seeks a privacy he has not found in Galilee. He plans to teach his disciples. But even here, in out-or-the-way Tyre, he cannot escape the interruption of human need.

1.   When we take time off to "get away" from our routine, why is easy to get away from our core values as well?

The woman who comes to Jesus is called a "Syrophoenician" by Mark (vs. 26) and a "Canaanite" by Matthew (15:22). Mark seems to be describing her political background, while Matthew highlights the fact that she is from a race disowned by orthodox Jews. This story must be seen in view of the vast differences that exist between her and Jesus. Her faith shines brightly as she overcomes imposing barriers:

The Unfamiliar Barrier — This woman lives in a region where Jesus is a stranger. Most likely she has only heard of his power and compassion. Her concern is for her daughter and has probably taken her down many blind alleys and to many dead end cures. But she is a desperate mother, driven to continue to try. And so, moved by her love for her daughter, she begs for help from this stranger.

2.   Is it easy for you to talk to strangers? Why or Why not?

3.   How easily do past disappointments stifle your determination to keep trying?

4.   Why do we want to stay with those who are like us?

The Racial Barrier — Racial discrimination by Jews was well known among Gentiles. In fact, Gentiles were commonly referred to as "dogs." And so, in his testing, Jesus is in effect, saying: "I am a Jew! What makes you think that a Gentile, can get a blessing from a Jewish prophet?!" But, even in the face of this apparent insult, her need persists, and so she persists.

5.   What kind of insult does it take to make your humility vanish?

The Pride Barrier — In humility she uses Jesus' own words to repeat her request. She says, in effect, that she needs even the crumbs. It is this awareness of our own need that opens a way for God to work in our lives (cf. Mt 5:3). But it is not just humility that the Syrophoenician woman demonstrates. She also shows confidence!

6.   What does she teach us about taking needs to God (Heb. 4:15-16)?

The Faith Barrier — Jesus tells her to go home to a cured daughter. But after so many blind alleys, can it be true? Can she trust his promise and act in faith? Or is he simply trying to finally get rid of her? She overcomes her last barrier and, in faith, goes home.

7.   What is trusting faith? How does it show itself? What does it do?

24 Jesus left that place and went to the vicinity of Tyre. He entered a house and did not want anyone to know it; yet he could not keep his presence secret. 25 In fact, as soon as she heard about him, a woman whose little daughter was possessed by an evil spirit came and fell at his feet. 26 The woman was a Greek, born in Syrian Phoenicia. She begged Jesus to drive the demon out of her daughter. 27 "First let the children eat all they want," he told her, "for it is not right to take the children's bread and toss it to their dogs." 28 "Yes, Lord," she replied, "but even the dogs under the table eat the children's crumbs." 29 Then he told her, "For such a reply, you may go; the demon has left your daughter." 30 She went home and found her child lying on the bed, and the demon gone.

My Thoughts Today …

Read Mark 7:31-37

Jesus leaves the region of Tyre and Sidon and moves 40 miles back down to the southeast coast of the Sea of Galilee. On a map this route is obviously very long and difficult. Mark sums it up in one sentence, but actually, the trip might have taken several weeks. Jesus might be giving Herod Antipas a wide berth. But he is more likely still seeking seclusion where he can teach and prepare his disciples.

It is significant that the residents of the Decapolis area, who had once begged Jesus to leave their region (5:17), now beg him to stay. Apparently the demoniac (5:19-20) has been a convincing messenger. His thankfulness could not be contained!

1.   Are you a thankful person? How does it show itself in your life?

2.   How can your thankfulness be more evident to others?

Jesus encounters a man whose condition is described with the word "stammerer," which is used only here and in Isaiah 35:6, where it explains how "the tongue of the dumb [will] shout for joy" when the Messiah comes. According to Isaiah, the Messiah was expected to open blind eyes and free dumb lips (29:18; 32:3f.; 42:7; 61:1). Jesus has been fulfilling this Messianic ministry for some time and the news about him continues to spread.

Faithful Friends — Parallel to the story of the paralytic (2:1-12), a group of people now bring a deaf and dumb man to Jesus. In both stories several friends act together on behalf of a mutual sick friend. They show that faith is often plural. This is still true today. Very few people come to Jesus entirely on their own. Good friends, with faith, play a part … sometimes a very large part.

3.   Why do Christians today take their friends to Jesus?

4.   Who brought you to Jesus? Have you thanked them lately?

The Language of Touch — The detailed action by Jesus is to be expected. The man is unable to even ask for help. And so it is natural for Jesus to communicate his intentions with signs rather than words. He takes time with the man because he wants him to understand. Jesus speaks a universal language that even this man can understand — the language of touch !

5.   Why is the human touch so rare today?

6.   What is the real power of touch? What makes it phony or selfish?

The Sound Of Compassion — The feeling churning inside of Jesus is expressed as a deep, exhausting "sigh" (vs. 34). It is a sympathetic sensitivity that he has known many times when faced with human suffering. It is his yearning toward God that feels the misery and the distress of the man. It is the sound of compassion.

7.   Why does our culture often shield itself from real pity? How does it do this?

8.   How often and how deeply do you allow yourself to really "feel" the pain of others?

9.   How can you move from "feeling" to "deciding" to "acting"?

Mark 7:31-37

31 Then Jesus left the vicinity of Tyre and went through Sidon, down to the Sea of Galilee and into the region of the Decapolis. 32 There some people brought to him a man who was deaf and could hardly talk, and they begged him to place his hand on the man. 33 After he took him aside, away from the crowd, Jesus put his fingers into the man's ears. Then he spit and touched the man's tongue. 34 He looked up to heaven and with a deep sigh said to him, "Ephphatha!" (which means, "Be opened!"). 35 At this, the man's ears were opened, his tongue was loosened and he began to speak plainly. 36 Jesus commanded them not to tell anyone. But the more he did so, the more they kept talking about it. 37 People were overwhelmed with amazement. "He has done everything well," they said. "He even makes the deaf hear and the mute speak."

My Thoughts Today ...

Read Mark 8:1-10

What can the witness of one man do? Consider the rapid spread of excitement, through the Decapolis region, over the healing of a deaf mute (7:31-37). In a region once very closed to Jesus (5:17), this sudden gathering of 4,000 people, now very open to his teaching, can be traced back to one man — the healed demoniac (5:20). The hard hearts of earlier days are now soft and responsive (cf. 4:4, 15).

1. Reflect on how God can work through one life to reach many lives.

2. What are examples of this today?

3. How has he and how can he work through your life?

At first glance, this story looks very much like the feeding of the 5,000 (6:30-46). Some commentators even say too much so. But consider these important differences:

Gentile Soil — Earlier Mark told the story of the feeding of 5,000 Jews. But the 4,000 here are clearly Gentiles. Even the basket used to collect the leftovers, sphuris (vs. 8), is the large hamper-like basket of the common Gentile peasant. In contrast, the basket used earlier was the smaller Jewish lunch basket, kaphinos (6:43). This Gentile mission demonstrates that even though Jesus' ministry began with his own people (Mt 15:24), his eventual mission is to all people (Mk 11:17). The two feeding stories demonstrate a truth later described by Paul. He will write that God's offering of salvation is "for the Jew, then for the Gentile" (Ro 1:16). He will explain that, in view of God's ultimate mission, "there is no difference between Jew and Gentile . . . everyone who calls on the name of the Lord will be saved" (Ro 10:12-13).

4. How narrow or broad is the scope of your ministry?

5. What is the most difficult kind of person for you to relate to?

6. How will God reach this person? Who will he send? Could he send you?

Different Motive — In both feedings Jesus is moved with "compassion." Earlier he was moved because he saw a desperate search for Jewish leadership, even though it was misguided (6:34). Now he is moved because, in their eagerness to hear his teaching, this Gentile crowd has been without food for a long time (vs. 2). Jesus is sensitive to all needs and responds to every human pain. So, after feeding their souls, he now feeds them bread and fish.

7. What restricts our view of human need?

8. How can we broaden our awareness and our response?

Three Days — Jesus does not assume that this Gentile crowd needs the same kind of teaching that he had earlier given the 5,000 Jews. During the encounter with the Jews, his boat trip, the feeding and the teaching took place all in one day (6:32-44). But in this encounter, he spends all of three days just teaching.

9. How can we, like Jesus, be more discerning, flexible and specific?

10. How can we meet both felt and ultimate needs?

1 During those days another large crowd gathered. Since they had nothing to eat, Jesus called his disciples to him and said, 2 "I have compassion for these people; they have already been with me three days and have nothing to eat. 3 If I send them home hungry, they will collapse on the way, because some of them have come a long distance." 4 His disciples answered, "But where in this remote place can anyone get enough bread to feed them?" 5 "How many loaves do you have?" Jesus asked. "Seven," they replied. 6 He told the crowd to sit down on the ground. When he had taken the seven loaves and given thanks, he broke them and gave them to his disciples to set before the people, and they did so. 7 They had a few small fish as well; he gave thanks for them also and told the disciples to distribute them. 8 The people ate and were satisfied. Afterward the disciples picked up seven basketfuls of broken pieces that were left over. 9 About four thousand men were present. And having sent them away, 10 he got into the boat with his disciples and went to the region of Dalmanutha.

My Thoughts Today ...

Read Mark 8:11-21

The demand for a miracle follows Jesus all through his public ministry. Even at his death he hears the taunt "Come down ... and save yourself" (15:30-32). But he never gives in. His power has a clear purpose — to relieve suffering and point people to God. But, true to form, the Pharisees meet Jesus on the western shore demanding "proof" that he is the Messiah. And why not! Others came with big public relations programs. Like Theudas (Ac 5:36) who, according to Josephus (Ant. 20.5.1), promised to divide the Jordan. And so, Jesus is expected to "prove" that he is the Messiah. The appeal has two sides to it:

Political Pride — Since Satan had first suggested that Jesus "show off" in the most visible place in Jerusalem, the pinnacle of the temple (Mt 4:5-6), there has been a constant pressure for Jesus to make a political name for himself. But he resists. He stays true to his Father's mission.

1.   Jesus could easily meet all expectations and become a powerful political Messiah — but how would this change his God-given mission?

Fabulous Faith — Jesus also refuses to dazzle people into faith … providing signs for their own sake. If the evidence of his teaching, his healing and his life are not convincing then, as he says, "no sign will be given" (vs. 12) (cf. Lk 16:31). What "evidence" in Jesus are the Pharisees overlooking?

Jesus uses the example of yeast to picture a powerful influence for good or for bad (cf. Mt 13:3). He is concerned that his disciples are not being misled. Notice his warning:

The Yeast Of The Pharisees — The legalistic human demands of the Pharisees miss the heart of God as they search for perfection through human effort. Jesus wants his disciples to rely on God and find their security there.

The Yeast Of Herod — This kind of worldly ambition obviously pulls at the Twelve (cf. 10:35-45). It is a problem Jesus will have to address again and again.

2.   Why are the Twelve so susceptible to outside influences?

3.   What is most likely to influence you for bad?

After watching Jesus teach, heal and feed 9,000 people, the disciples should begin to recognize who he is. But they "don't understand."

After teaching by the lake — "Don't you understand this parable?" (4:13)

After the storm — "Why are you so afraid? Have you still no faith?" (4:40)

After feeding 5,000 — "Had not understood ... their minds were closed" (6:52)

After feeding 4,000 — "Do you still not see or understand? Are your hearts hardened? Do you have eyes but fail to see, and ears and fail to hear? And don't you remember?… Do you still not understand?" (8:17-21)

Their perception is clouded with misunderstanding. Their senses are dull to his words. Jesus keeps giving them the picture. But they keep losing it.

4.   The disciples do not see or hear completely. Why?

5.   What in Jesus is difficult for you to see and understand?

11 The Pharisees came and began to question Jesus. To test him, they asked him for a sign from heaven. 12 He sighed deeply and said, "Why does this generation ask for a miraculous sign? I tell you the truth, no sign will be given to it." 13 Then he left them, got back into the boat and crossed to the other side. 14 The disciples had forgotten to bring bread, except for one loaf they had with them in the boat. 15 "Be careful," Jesus warned them. "Watch out for the yeast of the Pharisees and that of Herod." 16 They discussed this with one another and said, "≠It is because we have no bread." 17 Aware of their discussion, Jesus asked them: "Why are you talking about having no bread? Do you still not see or understand? Are your hearts hardened? 18 Do you have eyes but fail to see, and ears but fail to hear? And don't you remember? 19 When I broke the five loaves for the five thousand, how many basketfuls of pieces did you pick up?" "Twelve," they replied. 20 "And when I broke the seven loaves for the four thousand, how many basketfuls of pieces did you pick up?" They answered, "Seven." 21 He said to them, "Do you still not understand?"

My Thoughts Today …

Read Mark 8:22-26

After grieving the disciples' inability to "see" (7:17-21), Jesus now meets a man who, more than anything else, wants to see. In the Old Testament prophets, the opening of blind eyes, the freeing of mute tongues and the unstopping of deaf ears were signs of the arrival of the Day of the Lord.

> *In that day the deaf will hear the words of the scroll,*
> *and out of gloom and darkness the eyes of the blind will see.*
> *Isaiah 29:18*
> *cf. 32:3f; 35:5; 42:7*

> *At that time (day) your mouth will be opened;*
> *you will speak with him and will no longer be silent.*
> *So you will be a sign to them, and they will know that I am the Lord.*
> *Ezekiel 24:27*

1.   Why is it significant that this story, of helping someone to see, follows a story of the disciples' inability to see (8:11-21)?

2.   In what areas of life and truth do you now "see" more clearly?

3.   How did God help your vision to clear?

Blindness is the issue. But this miracle is the only one in the gospels that describes a gradual cure, in two stages. In stage one sight returns, but not completely. He can distinguish objects, but they are blurred. It is only after a second touch that the cure is complete and the man's picture sharpens. Since Jesus could have healed the man instantly, and does in every other incident, what does this story mean?

Lost Vision — For Jesus, blindness is often a symbol of lost spiritual or moral sight (Mt 23:24,26; Lk 6:39; Eph 4:18). It was also a common metaphor in the Old Testament (I Sa 12:3). Perhaps this is why Jesus will at times mix a story of real blindness with a message of spiritual blindness (Jn 9:1-41).

> *For judgment I have come into this world,*
> *so that the blind will see and those who see will become blind.*
> *John 9:39*

Enacted Parable — The Old Testament prophets often acted out their message, sometimes dramatically. For example, the marriage of Hosea to the prostitute Gomer was a message of God's enduring love for an unfaithful Israel. This kind of symbolic action was widespread in the Old Testament and very familiar to the Jews of Jesus' day. So, on this day in Bethsaida, when Jesus heals a blind man, he mixes in a dramatic message for his disciples. It is a parable of hard hearts, half opened eyes and immature faith that is slowly awakening.

4.   What is unclear to you about Jesus or his mission?

5.   What about him do you resist?

6.   Ask him now to help you see more clearly.

22 They came to Bethsaida, and some people brought a blind man and begged Jesus to touch him. 23 He took the blind man by the hand and led him outside the village. When he had spit on the man's eyes and put his hands on him, Jesus asked, "Do you see anything?" 24 He looked up and said, "I see people; they look like trees walking around." 25 Once more Jesus put his hands on the man's eyes. Then his eyes were opened, his sight was restored, and he saw everything clearly. 26 Jesus sent him home, saying, "Don't go into the village."

My Thoughts Today ...

Read Mark 8:27-30

    The city-state of Caesarea Philippi was formerly known as Paneas after Pan, the god of the fields. It was rebuilt by Herod Philip in honor of the Roman emperor and was therefore called "Philip's Caesarea" or Caesarea Philippi. Since it is outside Galilee, it is a good place for Jesus to travel in order to think and to talk.

1.   Why does traveling often make it easier for people to think and talk?

2.   Reflect on the last important talk you had "on the way" (vs. 27).

    Jesus has been quiet about who he is for a long time. He knows that words can fail because they require the listener to have "ears to hear." Talking his identity can be very dangerous. So, for months he has worked hard at living his identity. And though the Twelve have seen him give his time and energy, they have not seen his ultimate goal (8:17-21). They have not seen how his serving style leads directly to the highest form of service — self sacrifice. Like the blind man (8:1-10), they need a second touch. So Jesus raises the issue that they have been pondering all along:

    John / Elijah / Prophet — The theories and rumors about Jesus are varied and flattering stretching from the distant Elijah to the more recent John the Baptist. And the opinions are all championed for the same political, material or personal reasons. For centuries the Jews have waited for their political Messiah and the return of the "kingdom" with all its glory and power. The Twelve are probably excited just to be in on the ground floor.

3.   If we took a poll today, what would people say about Jesus?

4.   What kind of motives do people have for following Jesus today?

5.   How can you test or examine your own motives?

    Messiah — Peter says what the others are too timid to say. He knows who Jesus is! The Greek title "Christ" and its Hebrew counter-part "Messiah" mean "anointed one." They point back to the time when God's "anointed" ruled the nation as commander in chief. It is the military and political overtones of this title that explain why Jesus has not used it … and why Peter uses it now.

6.   How can Peter be with Jesus for so long and still misunderstand him?

    Jesus Warned Them — The Jews have always regarded the greatest days in their history as the days of king David. He had been an "anointed one" who ruled with power, wealth and honor. And the Jews of Jesus' day dream that another king will come from David's line. He will be a Messiah and a warlord who will re-establish Israel with power (Isa 9:7; Jer 23:5; 30:9). But their ideas are violent, destructive and vengeful. It's no wonder Jesus works so hard to redefine them. It's no wonder he focuses on living his identity for the Twelve to see. It's no wonder he warns them not to tell who they think he is. They correctly call him "Messiah" but they have no idea what the title really means.

7.   If the Twelve, living with Jesus for three years misunderstand him, how might we, 2,000 years removed, misunderstand him?

Mark 8:27-30

27 Jesus and his disciples went on to the villages around Caesarea Philippi. On the way he asked them, "Who do people say I am?" 28 They replied, "Some say John the Baptist; others say Elijah; and still others, one of the prophets." 29 "But what about you?" he asked. "Who do you say I am?" Peter answered, "You are the Christ." 30 Jesus warned them not to tell anyone about him.

My Thoughts Today ...

Read Mark 8:31-38

Peter reveals that he believes that Jesus is the long awaited political Messiah. He is a king in disguise. He is a rebel leader, who will throw off Roman tyranny and re-establish God's people as an independent state. But at the very moment that Peter answers "Messiah," Jesus begins to teach them, not about a victorious political king but about a son of man, who must undergo great suffering, rejection and death.

Jesus Spoke Plainly (vs. 31-32) — Jesus' direction is clear and his purpose is certain. Notice the "must" in verse 31. He speaks "plainly" — perhaps a little too plainly for some. But those who follow must understand whom they are following and where he is really going. This is the staggering disclosure for which Jesus has been preparing his disciples. He is the Messiah. He is the king. But his glory will not be found on a Jewish throne, but on a Roman cross.

1.   Why does Jesus wait until now to speak so "plainly" about his cross and his death?

2.   How can Christians today be as certain of their life purpose?

3.   Are most people in the world this sure of their direction? Are you?

Peter Rebuked (vs. 32) — Peter has always thought of the Messiah in terms of irresistible conquest. And in Jesus he sees his own place in a victorious conquering force. So it must be confusing to hear Jesus talk about suffering and death. Peter can't imagine how "Messiah" could ever be connected to defeat and death. What is inevitable for Jesus, is unthinkable for Peter.

4.   How would you handle it if your faith was challenged by a friend?

Of God … Of Men (vs. 33) — From Peter's lips Jesus recognizes a tempting voice that he has heard before (Mt 4:8-11). It is a terrible thing when a well-meaning, but misguided friend becomes a tool of Satan. So, as he did earlier in the wilderness, Jesus again refuses a worldly kingdom. And at the same time he challenges Peter to consider whose dream he is really following — God's or Satan's.

5.   Like Jesus we have two options: God's way or the world's way. How would you describe the difference?

6.   Today, why do so many choose the world's way (Mt 7:13-14)?

Come After Me (vs. 34) — Self-denial and the cross are the language of discipleship. To follow Jesus is to budget for the loss of your own life. But Jesus is not saying that you should deny your self-worth, or to deny yourself joy or food or marriage etc. (cf. 1 Ti 4:3-5). Instead, self-denial means that God is now caring for your self. It is no longer your task. Someone much better is on the job! In fact, the best way to care for your own soul is to put it into the hands of God (vs. 35-37).

7.   How do people misunderstand "self-denial" today?

8.   Being relieved of the task of self-promotion frees us for what?

9.   What does it mean to take up your cross and follow Jesus?

31 He then began to teach them that the Son of Man must suffer many things and be rejected by the elders, chief priests and teachers of the law, and that he must be killed and after three days rise again. 32 He spoke plainly about this, and Peter took him aside and began to rebuke him. 33 But when Jesus turned and looked at his disciples, he rebuked Peter. "Get behind me, Satan!" he said. "You do not have in mind the things of God, but the things of men." 34 Then he called the crowd to him along with his disciples and said: "If anyone would come after me, he must deny himself and take up his cross and follow me. 35 For whoever wants to save his life will lose it, but whoever loses his life for me and for the gospel will save it. 36 What good is it for a man to gain the whole world, yet forfeit his soul? 37 Or what can a man give in exchange for his soul? 38 If anyone is ashamed of me and my words in this adulterous and sinful generation, the Son of Man will be ashamed of him when he comes in his Father's glory with the holy angels."

My Thoughts Today …

What I Learned This Week ...

... About Jesus

... About Ministry

... About Myself

Day 43
9:1-8

Day 44
9:9-13

Day 45
9:14-29

Day 46
9:30-32

Week 7   *The Transition*
Day 43-49   *Mark 9:1-50*

Day 47
9:33-37, 10:13-16

Day 48
9:38-41

Day 49
9:42-50

The Transition

Mark 9:1-50

This week, as you walk with Jesus, you will see him come down from an encouraging mountain top experience into a valley of arguing. Watch him prepare to pass the baton of ministry by spending special time alone with his disciples.

As he uses children to prepare the Twelve to carry his ministry forward, look for the childlike quality most needed in your own life.

My Prayer For This Week …

Read Mark 9:1-8

A week after Peter's confession and conflict with Jesus comes this dramatic Transfiguration event. It is very difficult to describe since it is completely foreign to any normal human experience. It probably takes place on one spur of the 9,200 foot Mount Hermon, twelve miles from Caesarea Philippi (8:27). Compared to the usual light from a candle or a lamp, the "dazzling white" of Jesus is overwhelming and indescribable. The Transfiguration has a double significance:

First For Jesus — Notice the parallel with events from the beginning of his ministry. He has just endured another temptation experience by Satan/Peter (8:33), a grim reminder of the former test (Mt 4:1-10). And now, as in the beginning (1:11), he is reminded, in a heavenly voice that he is God's son and that he is loved (9:7). He is further encouraged by Moses and Elijah who talk with him about his future death (Lk 9:31).

1.   Why does God affirm and encourage Jesus at this point in the story?

Second For The Disciples — Jesus knows that discipleship for the Twelve will become more and more difficult. He knows their weak points. He knows their needs. Notice his deliberate style.

> *Jesus took Peter, James and John ... [He] led them ...*
> *They were all alone ... transfigured before them.*

It is no accident that Jesus singles these men out. As the most outspoken of the Twelve, these three need this Transfiguration message the most. It is a message from God himself. Try to see the scene from their point of view:

· They See Jesus — He is with two of the greatest men of Israel's past, Moses and Elijah, representing the Law and the Prophets. Both ended their lives in mysterious ways (Dt 34:6; 2 Ki 2:11). But more importantly, to any patriotic Jew, it is suspected that either might return to lead the Jews back to political power (Dt 18:18; Mal 4:5)!

· They See A Cloud Descend — This is an old signal of the presence and the leadership of God (Ex 16:10; 19:9; 24:15-16; 33:9; Lev 16:2; Nu 11:25; 1 Ki 8:10).

· They Hear God's Voice — God says listen to Jesus, and suddenly Jesus is alone. Mark even uses a double negative to communicate that Moses and Elijah are clearly gone from the picture. Also, the word "suddenly" carries the meaning "unexpectedly." The disciples are surprised. They do not expect Moses and Elijah to be taken away.

The message is clear. God himself speaks to their political preoccupation. First he creates their political dream, including three of their messianic heroes — Jesus, Moses and Elijah. Then, with their political hopes and dreams in full bloom (vs. 5), he pours cold water on them by "suddenly" taking Moses and Elijah away and saying "THIS is my son" and in effect saying, "you are not listening to him."

2.   What preoccupation is most likely to keep you from seeing God's mission?

3.   God was dramatic. He wanted them to put aside their dream and listen to his dream. What does it usually take to get you to listen?

1 And he said to them, "I tell you the truth, some who are standing here will not taste death before they see the kingdom of God come with power." 2 After six days Jesus took Peter, James and John with him and led them up a high mountain, where they were all alone. There he was transfigured before them. 3 His clothes became dazzling white, whiter than anyone in the world could bleach them. 4 And there appeared before them Elijah and Moses, who were talking with Jesus. 5 Peter said to Jesus, "Rabbi, it is good for us to be here. Let us put up three shelters — one for you, one for Moses and one for Elijah." 6 (He did not know what to say, they were so frightened.) 7 Then a cloud appeared and enveloped them, and a voice came from the cloud: "This is my Son, whom I love. Listen to him!" 8 Suddenly, when they looked around, they no longer saw anyone with them except Jesus.

My Thoughts Today ...

Read Mark 9:9-13

Throughout Jewish history, the mountains were frequently the place where God revealed himself (Ex 24; 34; 1 Ki 18:20; 19:8, 11). With this background in mind, it stands to reason that the three disciples are thinking hard about their encounter with God as they come down from Mount Hermon. Many things puzzle them:

The Charge to not reveal the Messiah they have found in Jesus (8:30).

The Prediction of death which crushes their kingdom hopes (8:31).

The Transfiguration of Jesus in dazzling white (9:3).

The Voice booming from heaven (9:7).

Jesus reads their confusion and asks them to tell no one what they have seen until after his death and resurrection. He can see that they still do not understand what messiahship really means. He knows that the only thing that will unseat their violent desire to unleash God's force, is to see for themselves the crucifixion of God's love (cf. Jn 12:32).

1.　What is the power of martyrdom and self-sacrifice?

2.　How will the death of Jesus finally instruct the disciples?

The discussion about Elijah is probably prompted by his appearance at the Transfiguration. There has been a lot of talk about Elijah's expected return. It is thought that he will precede the Messiah's coming (Lk 1:17). Two verses in the Old Testament have planted these seeds of expectation:

> *See, I will send you the prophet Elijah*
> *before that great and dreadful day of the Lord comes.*
> *He will turn the hearts of the fathers to their children,*
> *and the hearts of the children to their fathers;*
> *or else I will come and strike the land with a curse.*
> *Malachi 4:5-6*

Everyone expects Elijah to be the introduction to this special "day" when God's Messiah restores Israel to power. So, as they descend from Mount Hermon, Jesus explains that Elijah has come back. But, he quickly turns their attention from the exciting Transfiguration of Elijah to the hard facts of the death of John the Baptist, Jesus' actual forerunner. He brings their vision "down to earth" by again facing them with the picture of suffering & death.

Yes, John is functioning in an Elijah role, but as Elijah had Jezebel, so John had Herodias (1 Ki 19:2; Mk 6:24). Jesus keeps on upsetting their ideas about God's kingdom. They are looking for the Forerunner, then the Messiah and finally the long awaited National State of Israel.

So, using their own step by step view of things, Jesus says in effect, "The forerunner has been executed, the Messiah will be crucified and your political dream is not in the plan."

3.　What are preconceived ideas?

4.　Identify some that you see today?

5.　Why are they often dangerous to God's kingdom?

9 As they were coming down the mountain, Jesus gave them orders not to tell anyone what they had seen until the Son of Man had risen from the dead. 10 They kept the matter to themselves, discussing what "rising from the dead" meant. 11 And they asked him, "Why do the teachers of the law say that Elijah must come first?" 12 Jesus replied, "To be sure, Elijah does come first, and restores all things. Why then is it written that the Son of Man must suffer much and be rejected? 13 But I tell you, Elijah has come, and they have done to him everything they wished, just as it is written about him."

My Thoughts Today ...

Read Mark 9:14-29

We all know that often after every mountain-top experience there comes a valley. And in Jesus' case, the heavenly experience of Mount Hermon is quickly followed by the human experience in this valley of anguish and arguing. The temptation for him to stay on the mountain must be great. His words "how long shall I stay with you" (vs. 19) almost sound homesick.

1. Why does Jesus stay with his disciples?

Service is of a higher quality if it is strengthened by retreat. But retreat is only meaningful if it leads back to service. Jesus is at odds with his disciples on this point. They want to build tents on the mountain top to enjoy God. But Jesus chooses to return to human need to serve God.

2. Is your faith more heroic on the mountain or in the valley?

3. What is lacking in a retreat that doesn't prepare us to serve?

In the valley, Jesus finds both the evil of possession, and the evil of faithlessness:

Misplaced Faith — While Jesus is on the mountain with Peter, James and John, the other disciples are in the valley arguing about the demon possessed boy. It is sad that this boy could be important to the disciples only as a notch on their gun or a sign of their success. Are they confident in God's power (6:7) or in their own?

4. Why do some deny their failure, while others accept it and seek help?

Rejected Faith — The "teachers of the law" are probably happy that Jesus' disciples cannot help the young boy. They are not as concerned with a young boy's health as they are with discrediting Jesus and his disciples.

5. Have you ever been happy that someone failed to do good? Why?

6. Where does this attitude come from? (cf. 1 Co 13:6)

Incomplete Faith — The father of the boy has come looking for Jesus, but instead, he finds the disciples. Consider how discouraging it is to come looking for sensitivity, only to find selfishness. Perhaps this is why he says, "If you can do anything" (vs. 22). This father has a small faith and knows that he needs more. His statement, "help me overcome my unbelief" (vs. 24) is the cry of a faith struggling to be born. And though it is incomplete, Jesus honors his humble and dependent attitude.

7. What is incomplete in your faith?

8. Stop and pray the prayer of this father.

The most important lesson is stated in answer to the disciples question, "Why couldn't we drive it out?" Jesus replies, "This kind can come out only by prayer." (vs. 29). They had not prayed. Why? Because pride doesn't pray.

9. Do you see your service to others as God's gift or as your talent?

10. What is the difference?

11. Why doesn't pride pray?

14 When they came to the other disciples, they saw a large crowd around them and the teachers of the law arguing with them. 15 As soon as all the people saw Jesus, they were overwhelmed with wonder and ran to greet him. 16 "What are you arguing with them about?" he asked. 17 A man in the crowd answered, "Teacher, I brought you my son, who is possessed by a spirit that has robbed him of speech. 18 Whenever it seizes him, it throws him to the ground. He foams at the mouth, gnashes his teeth and becomes rigid. I asked your disciples to drive out the spirit, but they could not." 19 "O unbelieving generation," Jesus replied, "how long shall I stay with you? How long shall I put up with you? Bring the boy to me." 20 So they brought him. When the spirit saw Jesus, it immediately threw the boy into a convulsion. He fell to the ground and rolled around, foaming at the mouth. 21 Jesus asked the boy's father, "How long has he been like this?" "From childhood," he answered. 22 "It has often thrown him into fire or water to kill him. But if you can do anything, take pity on us and help us." 23 "'If you can'?" said Jesus. "Everything is possible for him who believes." 24 Immediately the boy's father exclaimed, "I do believe; help me overcome my unbelief!" 25 When Jesus saw that a crowd was running to the scene, he rebuked the evil spirit. "You deaf and mute spirit," he said, "I command you, come out of him and never enter him again." 26 The spirit shrieked, convulsed him violently and came out. The boy looked so much like a corpse that many said, "He's dead." 27 But Jesus took him by the hand and lifted him to his feet, and he stood up. 28 After Jesus had gone indoors, his disciples asked him privately, "Why couldn't we drive it out?" 29 He replied, "This kind can come out only by prayer."

My Thoughts Today ...

Read Mark 9:30-32

It is becoming clearer that Jesus is no longer the hero of Galilee and that the Herodian government is determined to kill him (Lk 13:31). After avoiding the political pressure of the 5,000 patriots (Mk 6:30-44), there are widespread desertions among Jesus' followers (Jn 6:66). In addition to this, opposition in the synagogues, which began as petty jealously, is now beginning to harden.

Passing Through Galilee — Not only is Jesus well known in Galilee, but anyone who knows him has a strong opinion about who he is and what he should be doing. There are a variety of views:

    · He should be king …

    · He should give in to the religious establishment …

    · He should teach more in line with the status quo …

    · He should quit stirring up trouble …

    · He should simply leave the area …

It is understandable why Jesus sticks to the back roads and crosses through Galilee in secret.

1.   After working with stubborn people, loving selfish people and staying with failing people, write down the kind of thoughts that must be going through Jesus' mind.

2.   Is he discouraged?

3.   How and why does he continue?

Teaching His Disciples — From the day he called them, Jesus has been concentrating more exclusively on the Twelve. In our day, religious leaders focus on their growing popularity and their opportunity to be "known" by larger and larger groups of people. But Jesus shows us the difference between simply impressing people and truly helping people. He causes us to ask what purpose it serves to mobilize crowds, if the individuals in the crowds have no personal supervision and instruction? Jesus shows that the way to reach the crowds is to focus on, and train, a few.

4.   If you only had three years to teach a person how to live a productive Christian life, what would you give them?

5.   Who are you doing this for now?

6.   Who is doing it for you?

Preparing To Leave — Jesus is preparing to leave. But, he isn't concentrating on getting his own affairs in order. Instead, he is making sure the disciples are ready for him to leave. He doesn't seem to have any purely personal concerns. His concerns are for others. His death will be both, at the hands of, and for the sake of, people. And his lifestyle of dying (to self and for people) is what Jesus wants the disciples to understand. This is his message and mission. And though he leaves his mission with them, he never leaves them.

7.   Why does genuine service include a desire to surrender self?

8.   What happens to "service" when sacrifice is removed from it?

30 They left that place and passed through Galilee. Jesus did not want anyone to know where they were, 31 because he was teaching his disciples. He said to them, "The Son of Man is going to be betrayed into the hands of men. They will kill him, and after three days he will rise." 32 But they did not understand what he meant and were afraid to ask him about it.

My Thoughts Today ...

Read Mark 9:33-37; 10:13-16

The basic meaning of the term "child" is small. This is the first observation when seeing a child standing near an adult. The child is smaller. We even get our English word "pauper" from the Greek term for child, paidon. A pauper has no means of support except charity. This was and is the state of a child — small, dependent, unable to make it in life alone.

The Greeks — In the early Greek world children were desired, especially sons. But with the Classical period began the practice of "exposing" unwanted children. Designed to weed out the unfit and unwanted, they literally took them and left them somewhere to die. The practice became so widespread that depopulation was the outcome (Polybius 36,17,7). Clearly the child was without power or significance.

The Jews — In all fairness, it must be said that Jewish parents loved and cared for their children. But a child's significance was determined by their future potential as an adult. Their value would come later, not now. And so, for a Rabbi, like Jesus, to spend time with a child was considered a waste of time. Consider this quote from Rabbi Jochanan:

> *Since the day the temple was destroyed,*
> *prophecy has been taken from the prophets*
> *and given to fools and children.*

One Of These Little Ones — For Jesus to spend time with children, and to say that we must be like children, moved totally against the grain of his day. It was to counter the pride of wanting to be great, that moved Jesus to use children to teach the apostles. With children, Jesus teaches about the kingdom, growth, true greatness and how to really hear God.

1.   **How does a little child "receive" something they truly need? (cf. 10:15)**

2.   **Why is there such a striving for greatness today?**

3.   **Why does rivalry not fit with a childlike character?**

Childlike or Childish — Exactly what kind of childlike character does Jesus mean? He can't be talking about the innocent child, or the humble child, or even the pure child because we have all known arrogant children and arrogant moments in every child. Every child is born childish, making demands and rarely saying "thank you." And who among us is innocent, humble and pure? Jesus is not talking about deserving the kingdom, but needing the kingdom. The child is destitute. The child is in desperate need. The child will die without help. This is Jesus' message of the child — needing God.

4.   **Read I Co 3:1-3.**

5.   **What is the difference between childlikeness and childishness?**

6.   **What is the first step in becoming like a child (cf. Jn 3:3)?**

7.   **What of childlikeness have you lost as you have grown older?**

33 They came to Capernaum. When he was in the house, he asked them, "What were you arguing about on the road?" 34 But they kept quiet because on the way they had argued about who was the greatest. 35 Sitting down, Jesus called the Twelve and said, "If anyone wants to be first, he must be the very last, and the servant of all." 36 He took a little child and had him stand among them. Taking him in his arms, he said to them, 37 "Whoever welcomes one of these little children in my name welcomes me; and whoever welcomes me does not welcome me but the one who sent me."

• • •

13 People were bringing little children to Jesus to have him touch them, but the disciples rebuked them. 14 When Jesus saw this, he was indignant. He said to them, "Let the little children come to me, and do not hinder them, for the kingdom of God belongs to such as these. 15 I tell you the truth, anyone who will not receive the kingdom of God like a little child will never enter it." 16 And he took the children in his arms, put his hands on them and blessed them.

My Thoughts Today ...

Read Mark 9:38-41

This episode obviously follows a time when Jesus was separated from the Twelve. They have been on their own for a while and now they want to tell him their story and measure their judgment. They seem sure that they have made the best decision and they want Jesus to confirm their confidence. But, in his judgement they come up short. In fact, it is almost inevitable that the proud, self-serving attitude of the Twelve would lead to the arrogant exclusiveness of this story.

1.   Why does pride always want to tell its story?

This is the only story in the Gospel of Mark where John is singled out to play a leading part. True to his nickname the "Son of Thunder" he shows his zealous intolerance (cf. Lk 9:54).

It was not unusual, in ancient times, for magicians or exorcists to utilize the name of some great person in their healings or exorcisms. In Galilee, the most likely setting for this story, Jesus is just such a great individual. And so, one day John overhears a rival exorcist using Jesus' name. John sees him as a rival because John is jealous.

2.   What is the power and the danger of jealousy?

As we will see later (10:35-45), the disciples are clearly jealous of each other's potential place in Jesus' kingdom, which they see as political. So they compete for positions of power among themselves. And though they are loyal to each other, it is a cliquish loyalty. They are proud of the special power Jesus has given them, and they are becoming more and more protective of the special relationship they have with him. Because of this, they want to limit the competition as much as possible. But notice Jesus' reaction:

"Do Not Stop Him" — It is natural for us to want others to embrace the same opinions and convictions that we have accepted. God's word is clear and there is no excuse for the extreme disunity that exists in belief and practice. But, in our search for truth, Jesus says to never oppose or hinder genuine service.

3.   Why are we sometimes threatened by the spiritual and humanitarian accomplishments of others?

"Not Against Us … For Us" — Jesus is not teaching neutrality of commitment here. He is not saying that it doesn't matter what you believe. It helps to compare this story with a second instance where Jesus uses similar language to make a different point, "He who is not with me, is against me" (Lk 11:23). In this second case the context is one of active hostility against Jesus. In such circumstances, Jesus says, neutrality is hostility — as in the case of Pilate remaining neutral as Jesus is sent to the cross. He was, in fact becoming involved in the hostility by refusing to oppose it.

Yes, it is true that everyone must take sides — for or against God. But here, in the context of Mark 9, Jesus is teaching that commitment to himself and hostility toward any good work cannot exist together.

4.   What is the difference between "neutrality" and "tolerance?"

5.   How is it possible to support the genuine service of those with whom you disagree?

38 "Teacher," said John, "we saw a man driving out demons in your name and we told him to stop, because he was not one of us." 39 "Do not stop him," Jesus said. "No one who does a miracle in my name can in the next moment say anything bad about me, 40 for whoever is not against us is for us. 41 I tell you the truth, anyone who gives you a cup of water in my name because you belong to Christ will certainly not lose his reward.

My Thoughts Today ...

Read Mark 9:42-50

Jesus knows that he will soon see Jerusalem and that his time of preparing the Twelve will end. The ministry will then be in their hands. And so, he is very stern and insistent about the heavy responsibilities that always accompany ministry:

Mill Stones — Drowning by millstone was a political warning. The Roman historian Suetonius (Augustus. 67), reports how the Zealots were killed in this manner during an uprising against Rome in AD 6. The Twelve have been preoccupied with a political agenda, so Jesus uses this well known warning to illustrate his own preoccupation — protecting and nourishing faith. Causing "one of these little ones … to sin" (vs. 42) stands in stark contrast to welcoming "one of these little children" (vs. 37). For Jesus, children symbolize humble, dependent faith, and are an important part of his teaching. You can almost hear the anger in this warning against misusing the power of influence.

1.   How would you describe the power of influence?

2.   How responsible do you feel for the spiritual growth of others?

Hell — Jesus not only cautions against leading others into sin, but also about being led into sin. And so he uses another familiar figure, "Gehenna" which is translated, "Hell." Literally, "valley of Hinnom." This ravine is south of Jerusalem and has long been the city's dump. As an open land-fill that constantly burned, this valley of filth and waste is associated with the destruction and punishment that awaits sinners.

Jesus uses graphic language. In fact, of the 12 occurrences of the term "hell" in the New Testament, eleven are from Jesus (Mt 5:22, 29, 30; 10:28; 18:9; 23:15, 33; Mk 9:43, 45, 47; Lk 12:5) and one is from his brother James (3:6). The language has to be so graphic because the stakes are so high. It is worth any sacrifice, any discipline and any self-denial to do the will of God.

3.   To avoid sin, what should be "cut out" of your life?

Salt — Jesus often uses proverbs which stick in the minds of people. Here he pictures the many uses of salt to illustrate a life of ministry:

· Being Salt — A disciple who has lost his zeal and devotion is like flat, bland salt. Jesus knows that the Twelve will soon have their zeal and devotion tested when he is taken and killed.

· Sharing Salt — With the incidents of quarreling fresh in his mind, Jesus knows that the Twelve must eventually learn to promote and nurture faith among themselves. And then they must learn to share that faith with others. But will they? With Jesus gone, will they be the "salt of the earth" (Mt 5:13).

4.   How can a Christian have a "preserving" influence in the world?

5.   What most easily dampens your zeal and your devotion?

42 "And if anyone causes one of these little ones who believe in me to sin, it would be better for him to be thrown into the sea with a large millstone tied around his neck. 43 If your hand causes you to sin, cut it off. It is better for you to enter life maimed than with two hands to go into hell, where the fire never goes out. 45 And if your foot causes you to sin, cut it off. It is better for you to enter life crippled than to have two feet and be thrown into hell. 47 And if your eye causes you to sin, pluck it out. It is better for you to enter the kingdom of God with one eye than to have two eyes and be thrown into hell, 48 where "'their worm does not die, and the fire is not quenched.' 49 Everyone will be salted with fire. 50 "Salt is good, but if it loses its saltiness, how can you make it salty again? Have salt in yourselves, and be at peace with each other."

My Thoughts Today ...

What I Learned This Week ...

... About Jesus

... About Ministry

... About Myself

Day 50
10:1-12

Day 51
10:17-23

Day 52
10:24-31

Day 53
10:32-34

Day 54
10:35-45

Day 55
10:46-52

Day 56
11:1-11

Week 8   The Journey
Day 50-56   Mark 10:1-11:11

The Journey

Mark 10:1-11:11

This week, as you walk with Jesus, you will see him turn south towards Jerusalem — the ultimate goal of his ministry on earth. But even as the group approaches the city of Jesus' death, watch the Twelve selfishly continue to follow their own political agenda.

Learn to avoid the schemes of the world as you take Jesus' mission as your own.

Read Mark 10:1-12

Jesus and the Twelve now turn south "and resolutely set out for Jerusalem" (Lk 9:51). They cross over to the Jordan river's east side and follow the southern route through Perea. This will be Jesus' final journey. Five different groups will come to Jesus with requests, criticisms and demands. Each will be absorbed in their own world. And no one but Jesus will see the climatic end of his life approaching.

1. How does it affect your forward progress when you receive criticism rather than encouragement and demands instead of help?

More and more, as he makes his way to Jerusalem, Jesus is confronted by his religious enemies. Divorce, as a topic, is not only hotly debated, it is also very dangerous. It had cost John the Baptist his life. The Pharisees want Jesus to say something about divorce that will allow them to incriminate him before Herod. After all, he has just entered Herod's territory. Perhaps the topic that killed John will also kill Jesus. The divorce discussion has two defective features:

It Focuses On Exceptions — The question they bring is not asking about God's intention but "What are the grounds for divorce?" One viewpoint (following Rabbi Hillel) allows husbands to divorce for a failure as minor as burnt food. Another viewpoint (following Rabbi Shammai) allows divorce only if the wife has been unfaithful. For both, the focus is on getting out, not on staying in.

It Is Unfairly One-Sided — According to Jewish thinking, a woman can commit adultery against her husband, but a man cannot commit adultery against his wife. He can only commit adultery against another married man. The standards are very one-sided.

The Pharisees try to pull Jesus into their "test" (cf. 8:11; 12:13). But he avoids their trap by speaking directly to their faulty focus:

Permanence — Moses' teaching (Dt 24:1-4) is not a statement of a positive law as much as it is a recognition of a negative problem. Jesus lifts the subject of marriage out of this legalistic context by highlighting the deeper principle of unbroken, lifelong commitment (Ge 1:27).

2. What happens to commitment if we begin to look for the exceptions?

Equality — Jesus places husband and wife in a relationship of equality by flatly contradicting the one-sided principle that a man cannot commit adultery against his own wife. According to Jesus both are to be faithful.

3. Do men still claim relational liberties not allowed to women?

4. Does our culture hold men less responsible for lust than women?

Oneness — Jesus reveals the intention of God. Marriage is more than a contract. It is a covenant. It is a commitment. It is not simply a man and woman living together. Instead, it is the fusion of two into one new person. Therefore, divorce doesn't simply end a contract. It breaks in half a single being.

5. How does the strength of oneness add to the pain of divorce?

6. How can a commitment to oneness strengthen a marriage?

Mark 10:1-12

1 Jesus then left that place and went into the region of Judea and across the Jordan. Again crowds of people came to him, and as was his custom, he taught them. 2 Some Pharisees came and tested him by asking, "Is it lawful for a man to divorce his wife?" 3 "What did Moses command you?" he replied. 4 They said, "Moses permitted a man to write a certificate of divorce and send her away." 5 "It was because your hearts were hard that Moses wrote you this law," Jesus replied. 6 "But at the beginning of creation God '≠made them male and female.' 7 'For this reason a man will leave his father and mother and be united to his wife, 8 and the two will become one flesh.' So they are no longer two, but one. 9 Therefore what God has joined together, let man not separate." 10 When they were in the house again, the disciples asked Jesus about this. 11 He answered, "Anyone who divorces his wife and marries another woman commits adultery against her. 12 And if she divorces her husband and marries another man, she commits adultery."

My Thoughts Today …

Read Mark 10:17-23

Each synoptic writer brings his own distinctive focus to this story. Only Luke (18:18) describes the man as a "Jewish leader." Only Matthew (19:20) describes him as "young." And only Mark (vs. 17) tells us that he "fell on his knees." This is not the first time someone has run to Jesus and fallen on their knees before him. Already Mark has told us about:

> · A lonely leper (1:40)
>
> · A tortured demoniac (5:6)
>
> · A worried father (5:22)
>
> · A desperate woman (5:33)
>
> · A determined mother (7:25)

All came to Jesus on their knees. All came aware of their needs. And all were helped by Jesus as he met their childlike dependency with support, challenge and direction. But this story is different. Like the others, it begins with the young man on his knees. But here the similarities end. This story is the only one in the gospels in which Jesus' command to follow is refused:

Flattery — The Jewish view is that God alone is "good" and to the degree that he is good, no one else is (I Ch 16:34; Ps 25:8; 34:8; 100:5; 118:1; Jer 33:11; Na 1:7). This explains Jesus' question (vs. 18). It is not simply a dispute about religious modesty. Jesus seems to be asking, "Is this just flattery, or do you understand that my goodness can only have one source — God?"

1. What motivates flattery?

2. What is usually hiding behind it?

Security — Notice that as Jesus answers the young man, he gives a carefully chosen partial listing of the Ten Commandments. He refers to the 6th, 7th, 8th, 9th and 5th commandments. They all apply to the young man's relationships with people. Jesus carefully omits the commandments dealing with the young man's relationship to God. Jesus is preparing him to face a fundamental weakness in his faith. He tells him "one thing you lack" (vs. 21). Then, he carefully and clearly tells the young man that he serves the wrong god. The sense of security that often characterizes the wealthy has become a barrier for this man. It has become his god. But, it is an insecure security. In contrast, those who are broken and deeply aware of their need are often closer to the kingdom than those who feel fulfilled and successful (2:17).

3. What creates an insecure security?

4. How does our culture promote a false sense of security?

5. Why is it so difficult for the comfortable and self-satisfied to enter the kingdom of God (vs. 24-25; cf. 4:18-19)?

Love — Jesus handles the young man directly and honestly. Mark calls the look Jesus gives him "love." It is not a look of anger or disgust, but a look of expectation, challenge and finally grief.

6. Why could this man not give up his wealth?

7. How could you make everything available to God (vs. 27)?

17 As Jesus started on his way, a man ran up to him and fell on his knees before him. "Good teacher," he asked, "what must I do to inherit eternal life?" 18 "Why do you call me good?" Jesus answered. "No one is good — except God alone. 19 You know the commandments: 'Do not murder, do not commit adultery, do not steal, do not give false testimony, do not defraud, honor your father and mother.'" 20 "Teacher," he declared, "all these I have kept since I was a boy." 21 Jesus looked at him and loved him. "One thing you lack," he said. "Go, sell everything you have and give to the poor, and you will have treasure in heaven. Then come, follow me." 22 At this the man's face fell. He went away sad, because he had great wealth. 23 Jesus looked around and said to his disciples, "How hard it is for the rich to enter the kingdom of God!"

My Thoughts Today ...

Read Mark 10:24-31

The disciples are startled by Jesus words. Like many they have always understood prosperity to be a sign of God's favor, while adversity indicates his disapproval (cf. Jn 9:1-3). But notice that Jesus does not condemn wealth or lift up poverty as virtuous. Instead, through a series of contrasts, he warns of the dangerous power of wealth and the joy of choosing another way.

Two Openings (vs. 25) — Jesus uses hyperbole, much like his plank/speck (Mt 7:3-5) and gnat/camel (Mt 23:24) stories. His point is graphic. To move a large animal through the eye of a needle is easier than trying to move through the door of the Kingdom with a huge sack of wealth strapped to your back.

1.   What is the addictive power of wealth?

2.   How does it become so firmly tied to our lives?

Two Powers (vs. 27) — With two simple phrases Jesus contrasts the impossible with the certain — "With Man" … "With God." In his lesson he seems to be saying that only God can give us the power to part with the wealth that distracts us and the possessions that separate us from the Kingdom.

3.   With God's help, what distraction should you begin to set aside?

Two Families (vs. 29-30) — Jesus honored his physical family but he also recognized and cherished his spiritual family (cf. 3:31-34). Many early Christians were disowned by their physical families because of their faith. But, as Jesus promises, and the early church later demonstrates, personal relationships are expanded and enriched by our spiritual family. Notice a few examples:

> *"His mother, who has been a mother to me" — Ro 16:13*
>
> *"In Christ Jesus I became your father" — 1 Co 4:15*
>
> *"The family of believers" — Gal 6:10*
>
> *"To Timothy my true son in the faith" — 1 Ti 1:2*
>
> *"To Titus, my true son in our common faith" — Tit 1:4*
>
> *"Exhort him as if he were your father. Treat younger men as brothers, older women as mothers, and younger women as sisters" — 1 Ti 5:1-2*
>
> *"Both the one who makes men holy and those who are made holy are of the same family. So Jesus is not ashamed to call them brothers" — Heb 2:11*

4.   How would you analyze the status of your two families?

Two Ages (vs. 30) — The faith that Jesus reveals, rooted in the Old Testament and filled out in the writings of the New Testament, is built upon two realities. He calls them "this present age" and "the age to come." We can call them time and eternity. Both are real and should be handled with careful planning.

5.   Many have a "now" plan, but how would you describe your "forever" plan?

6.   What are you doing in your life that will survive your death?

Two Positions (vs. 31) — In a surprising reversal of values, many will learn that what brings prominence on earth, does not in heaven (cf. Mt 20:16; Lk 13:30).

7.   For Jesus, what kinds of things count first in his kingdom?

24 The disciples were amazed at his words. But Jesus said again, "Children, how hard it is to enter the kingdom of God! 25 It is easier for a camel to go through the eye of a needle than for a rich man to enter the kingdom of God." 26 The disciples were even more amazed, and said to each other, "Who then can be saved?" 27 Jesus looked at them and said, "With man this is impossible, but not with God; all things are possible with God." 28 Peter said to him, "We have left everything to follow you!" 29 "I tell you the truth," Jesus replied, "no one who has left home or brothers or sisters or mother or father or children or fields for me and the gospel 30 will fail to receive a hundred times as much in this present age (homes, brothers, sisters, mothers, children and fields — and with them, persecutions) and in the age to come, eternal life. 31 But many who are first will be last, and the last first."

My Thoughts Today ...

Read Mark 10:32-34

The tension is thick. You can feel it hanging in the air as Jesus, his disciples and all of the other followers are steadily moving along:

· Their destination — "To Jerusalem"

· Jesus' attitude — "Leading the way"

· The disciple's attitude — "Afraid"

Jesus is sure of his destiny and relentless in his mission. The Twelve are apprehensive, lagging behind and almost defeated. In fact, the closer Jesus gets to his cross, the easier it is to see the difference between his mission and their mission.

Astonishment — "Jesus leading the way" (vs. 32) Picture the two groups. Jesus, a solitary figure, walking out ahead, and the disciples, astonished and afraid, but still following. Their fear is overruled by his determination. But they are still not sure what to do with Jesus' resolve. Even after all this time they continue to have trouble understanding his mission. But still, for all of their misunderstanding, they do love Jesus and continue to follow, even without understanding (cf. Jn 6:66-69).

1.　How complete of a picture do you require before you follow God?

2.　Describe the part love should play in faith.

Mission — "Again he took the Twelve aside" (vs. 32). Even as the picture grows darker, and he feels consumed with the task ahead (cf. Lk 12:50), Jesus remains true to his mission to train and equip the Twelve. The cross, his atoning death, is the absolute center of his mission. But that mission must be reproduced in the Twelve, or else it all ends at the cross.

3.　What happens if we understand and accept God's sacrificial love in our own lives, but then fail to pass it on to other lives? Whom are you equipping?

4.　What is most likely to keep you from passing your faith and your mission on to others?

Courage — "Mock him … spit on him … flog him … kill him" (vs. 34) Three times Jesus has predicted his death. And, with each consecutive announcement, the picture has become more horrible:

· 8:31 — He makes the first shocking announcement.

· 9:31 — He adds the tragedy of betrayal.

· 10:34 — He details the torture and ridicule.

With each step toward Jerusalem the future becomes clearer to Jesus. He continues only because of his courage. But his is not the impulsive kind of courage that appears only in an emergency when there is no time to think. His courage is much deeper. It looks far ahead and sees the hideous reality that is approaching. There have been many opportunities to turn back. Other options have been suggested by Satan, religious leaders, the Twelve and others. These alternatives would have ensured his popularity, his wealth and his safety. But instead, he goes on.

5.　Where does this kind of courage come from?

6.　What motivates it? How can it be developed by those who follow Jesus today?

32 They were on their way up to Jerusalem, with Jesus leading the way, and the disciples were astonished, while those who followed were afraid. Again he took the Twelve aside and told them what was going to happen to him. 33 "We are going up to Jerusalem," he said, "and the Son of Man will be betrayed to the chief priests and teachers of the law. They will condemn him to death and will hand him over to the Gentiles, 34 who will mock him and spit on him, flog him and kill him. Three days later he will rise."

My Thoughts Today …

Read Mark 10:35-45

How can this be happening? How can this request be made after Jesus has described in detail his approaching death? How can James and John be so insensitive, inconsiderate and self-serving? If there is any doubt that the Twelve misunderstand Jesus' mission, this story eliminates it. Three times he has described his death and three times they have missed his point. Like political party workers trying to arrange cabinet positions, James and John jealously ask for positions of power.

1. **Why is "position" so important to so many today?**

2. **How would you describe the dark side of ambition?**

3. **How does selfish ambition distort a mission of self-less serving?**

4. **How would you have answered such a selfish request for power?**

It is ironic that James and John ask to be on Jesus' Right and Left. In just a few days these positions will be taken, but not by James and John. Instead, they will be filled by crucified thieves.

It is clear that the "Sons of Thunder" do not know what they are asking. So, Jesus explains with two Jewish metaphors (vs. 38):

"Can You Drink The Cup?" — Very often, in the Old Testament, the cup was a symbol of suffering and punishment (Ps 75:8; Isa 51:17-22; Jer 25:15; Eze 23:31-34). And so, Jesus uses the cup imagery here, and at the last supper (14:23-24), and then again in his prayer in the garden (14:36).

5. **How does this story deepen your communion thoughts for "the cup?"**

"Can You Be Baptized?" — With a similar image, the metaphor of being overwhelmed in a flood of water was often used in the Old Testament to represent being overcome with distress and trouble (Ps 42:7; 69:2,15; 124:4; Isa 43:2). Earlier Jesus had said of his cross, "I have a baptism to undergo, and how distressed I am until it is completed!" (Lk 12:50). Jesus knows that in his cross he will be Submerged in trouble (Mk 14:33), Overwhelmed with sorrow (Mk 14:34) and Baptized into death (Ro 6:3).

6. **How do you usually cope when you feel overwhelmed by life?**

7. **What if you were submerged in the pain and sorrow of others?**

8. **At your own baptism (Ro 6) God placed the darkness of guilt and punishment upon Jesus. Take a few moments to thank him.**

Knowing that all twelve disciples are looking for political greatness (vs. 41), Jesus sits them down and contrasts their view of greatness with his own. Their goal is to be served (vs. 35). His is to serve (vs. 45).

Jesus states the meaning and purpose of his approaching death by connecting it to leadership and greatness. Alluding to Isaiah 53:11-12, he teaches that a great leader will lead by serving (cf. Jn 13:12-17). The theme of servanthood has been the map of Jesus' life. A great leader will do for others what they cannot do for themselves.

9. **Why does self-sacrifice attract and change lives (Jn 12:32-33)?**

10. **How does a serving style give a life credibility and authority?**

35 Then James and John, the sons of Zebedee, came to him. "Teacher," they said, "we want you to do for us whatever we ask." 36 "What do you want me to do for you?" he asked. 37 They replied, "Let one of us sit at your right and the other at your left in your glory." 38 "You don't know what you are asking," Jesus said. "Can you drink the cup I drink or be baptized with the baptism I am baptized with?" 39 "We can," they answered. Jesus said to them, "You will drink the cup I drink and be baptized with the baptism I am baptized with, 40 but to sit at my right or left is not for me to grant. These places belong to those for whom they have been prepared." 41 When the ten heard about this, they became indignant with James and John. 42 Jesus called them together and said, "You know that those who are regarded as rulers of the Gentiles lord it over them, and their high officials exercise authority over them. 43 Not so with you. Instead, whoever wants to become great among you must be your servant, 44 and whoever wants to be first must be slave of all. 45 For even the Son of Man did not come to be served, but to serve, and to give his life as a ransom for many."

My Thoughts Today ...

Read Mark 10:46-52

Jesus and his group cross the Jordan river and travel five miles west to Jericho. They are now ready to begin the fifteen mile uphill journey to Jerusalem. Jericho had been rebuilt by Herod the Great as his winter capital. It is an attractive town.

In Mark's story sometimes the blind have an amazing ability to "see" and the deaf often "hear" what everyone else misses. In this encounter with Blind Bartimaeus, Jesus once again mixed with this story of Real Blindness, a message of Spiritual Blindness:

Questions … Answers — It is probably no accident that Jesus asks the very question he had asked James and John in the last story, "What do you want me to do for you?" (vs. 36, 51). In both situations, Jesus seems to be asking:

"What do you think you need?"
"What do I have that you want?"

Jesus is not really drawing a comparison as much as a contrast. The questions are the same but the answers are vastly different. While James and John ask Jesus for positions of power, blind Bartimaeus simply wants to see.

1. Imagine Jesus asking you, "What do you want me to do for you?" How would you answer?

2. Would your answer look more like that of Bartimaeus or James and John?

Son of David — This is the only use of this title in the Gospel of Mark and it is used very near Jerusalem, the city of David. Jewish writings from around the time of Jesus (Psalms of Solomon 17:23), reveal that the cry "Son of David" is actually a salute to Jesus as the Messiah who has come to the city of king David as its new king (cf. Eze 34:20-24). Apparently the approach of Jesus with his disciples is seen as a political move. In fact, at the end of his fifteen mile journey, the solitary cry of Blind Bartimaeus will become the ovation of crowds shouting (11:1):

Blessed is the coming kingdom of our father David!

3. What must Jesus be thinking as he walks into this political time bomb?

Granted … Denied — Not only is the request of Bartimaeus different from that of James and John, but notice also that Jesus' response is different. While denying the young brothers their power, he gives Bartimaeus his sight. Why the difference? Perhaps because James and John came in pride and ignorance. Blind Bartimaeus comes in desperate need.

4. What keeps you from seeing your desperate need for God?

Need … Gratitude … Loyalty — Sometimes our need grows into selfishness as we move from desire to demand. Not so with Bartimaeus! When his need is met, it grows into gratitude which, in turn, leads to loyalty.

5. What happens to gratitude when it is not expressed?

6. What are you most thankful for? Offer a prayer of gratitude to God.

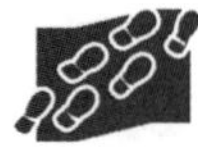

46 Then they came to Jericho. As Jesus and his disciples, together with a large crowd, were leaving the city, a blind man, Bartimaeus (that is, the Son of Timaeus), was sitting by the roadside begging. 47 When he heard that it was Jesus of Nazareth, he began to shout, "Jesus, Son of David, have mercy on me!" 48 Many rebuked him and told him to be quiet, but he shouted all the more, "Son of David, have mercy on me!" 49 Jesus stopped and said, "Call him." So they called to the blind man, "Cheer up! On your feet! He's calling you." 50 Throwing his cloak aside, he jumped to his feet and came to Jesus. 51 "What do you want me to do for you?" Jesus asked him. The blind man said, "Rabbi, I want to see." 52 "Go," said Jesus, "your faith has healed you." Immediately he received his sight and followed Jesus along the road.

My Thoughts Today …

Read Mark 11:1-11

Jerusalem has occupied the thoughts of Jesus for more than three years. As he walks the last 15 miles up from Jericho, he begins the last week of his life.

It is Passover time in Jerusalem. The Passover festival celebrates Israel's rescue from slavery (Ex 12:1ff). It always brings to mind Moses, God's champion in that ancient victory over Egyptian tyranny.

Today, Rome has replaced Egypt as the new oppressor and Jesus knows that the expectation that God will send another champion (Dt 18:18) is always in the minds of the pilgrims who have gathered in Jerusalem. The political tension is enormous. For him to enter Jerusalem now is certain to bring these patriotic feelings to a revolutionary boil:

Cloaks And Branches — An old memory is awakened as cloaks and branches are spread on the road. This is a conqueror's welcome, much like the celebration given Judas Maccabeus when he recaptured the temple from the Syrians in 163 BC (2 Maccabees 10:7) Is it possible that the crowds are expecting a new victory?

Hosanna — This is a politically charged term borrowed from Psalm 118:25. It simply means "Save Now!" It is a cry to God to save his people, now that their Messiah has come (cf. 2 Sa 14:4 and 2 Ki 6:26).

The Foal Of A Donkey — Contrast this scene and with the one in Jeremiah 22:4:

> *Kings who sit on David's throne*
> *will come through the gates of this palace,*
> *riding in chariots and on horses,*
> *accompanied by their officials and their people.*

For Jesus there is no white war horse. Instead he rides a donkey, the symbol of peace. The crowds must be puzzled by this Messiah who comes in peace without weapons and without an army.

1. **How do you usually respond to the expectations of others?**

2. **How do you feel when your convictions disappoint others?**

The atmosphere in the Temple is filled with dangerous tension, but there is no political explosion. Jesus simply inspects the Temple, then returns to Bethany. But, why does he enter the city only to turn around and leave? Notice how Jesus transforms what the crowd intended to be a Political Procession into his own Religious Pronouncement. Instead of attacking the Roman garrison as the crowd wanted, he leads the procession into the Temple. Instead of making speeches about Roman oppression, he seems to be saying:

> *Yes, I am a Messiah, but not a political one.*
> *Yes, I am leading a rebellion, but not against Rome.*
> *My attack is against what is really wrong, and I find it in your temple.*

3. **How does religion become corrupt?**

4. **From Jesus' example, how should we respond to corrupt religion?**

5. **Why are serious problems often more difficult to see when they occur in a religious setting?**

Mark 11:1-11

1 As they approached Jerusalem and came to Bethphage and Bethany at the Mount of Olives, Jesus sent two of his disciples, 2 saying to them, "Go to the village ahead of you, and just as you enter it, you will find a colt tied there, which no one has ever ridden. Untie it and bring it here. 3 If anyone asks you, 'Why are you doing this?' tell him, 'The Lord needs it and will send it back here shortly.'" 4 They went and found a colt outside in the street, tied at a doorway. As they untied it, 5 some people standing there asked, "What are you doing, untying that colt?" 6 They answered as Jesus had told them to, and the people let them go. 7 When they brought the colt to Jesus and threw their cloaks over it, he sat on it. 8 Many people spread their cloaks on the road, while others spread branches they had cut in the fields. 9 Those who went ahead and those who followed shouted, "Hosanna!" "Blessed is he who comes in the name of the Lord!" 10 "Blessed is the coming kingdom of our father David!" "Hosanna in the highest!" 11 Jesus entered Jerusalem and went to the temple. He looked around at everything, but since it was already late, he went out to Bethany with the Twelve.

My Thoughts Today ...

What I Learned This Week …

… *About Jesus*

… *About Ministry*

… *About Myself*

Day 57
11:12-25

Day 58
11:27-33

Day 59
12:1-12

Day 60
12:13-17

Day 61
12:18-27

Day 62
12:28-34

Day 63
12:35-37

Week 9   The City
Day 57-63   Mark 11:12-12:37

The City

Mark 11:12-12:37

This week, as you walk with Jesus through the city, feel the tension. Stand with Pharisees, Sadducees, Herodians, Temple authorities, and the crowds of pilgrims as Jesus speaks of the greatest commandment, the authority of ministry, and the defining image of God.

Watch his courage and then ask God to strengthen yours.

My Prayer For This Week ...

Read Mark 11:12-25

Having seen first hand the temple abuses the day before, Jesus is certain of what he must do. He begins the two mile trip back into the city of Jerusalem:

Cursing The Fruitless — This is Jesus' only negative miracle and it seems out of character for him. After all, it is too early to expect ripe figs. But look deeper:

· Parable — So far, Jesus has followed the habit of confronting unfruitful lives with creative agricultural parables:

> *Mt 7:19 — "Cut down and thrown in the fire."*
>
> *Lk 3:8 — "Fruit in keeping with repentance."*
>
> *Lk 13:31 — "Cut it down."*

And so, picking up some Old Testament imagery (Jer 8:13; Hos 9:10, 16-17; Joel 1:7; Mic 7:1ff), Jesus uses a fruitless tree to warn a fruitless Israel.

· Position — The cleansing of the temple is sandwiched in-between two parts of the fruitless tree story. The position of these stories paints a vivid picture of Israel's withering religion. Like the leaves of the tree promising fruit, Israel's appearance of faith is deceptive. And so, the words Jesus gives to the tree may be less of a curse than a simple statement of fact for Israel — "May no one ever eat fruit from you again." (cf. Ac 13:44-48).

1.   In what way did Jesus see Israel as barren and fruitless?

2.   What "fruit" does God expect from us — his "New Israel"?

Cleansing The Temple — Arriving in Jerusalem, Jesus goes immediately to the temple. There is no hesitation in his action. His plans are clear in his mind. More than a century earlier Judas Maccabeus had cleansed the temple of Gentiles. But now, Jesus cleanses it for Gentiles. As he clears the merchants and money-changers out of the "Court of the Gentiles" he once again reinterprets Messiahship. Part of the mission of the true Messiah is not to purge the country of the Romans, but to purge the temple of selfish commercialism. Jesus is angry with:

· The Exclusiveness — By reclaiming the Gentiles' area of worship, Jesus shows that God loves not only the Jew, but also the world (vs. 17).

· The Exploitation — Jesus rebukes the "Den of Robbers" for exploiting the worshippers for power and profit.

· The Desecration — The religious leaders have lost their sense of God's presence and are commercializing the Passover and the temple.

3.   What causes "exclusiveness" in religion today? What does it communicate to non-Christians?

4.   How has Christianity been commercialized? How can we preserve a sense of God's presence?

Making Enemies — Jesus never made a neutral impression on any person. Everyone either supported or opposed him. Here he reaffirms his earlier teaching that, "No one can serve two masters" (Mt 6:24). In doing so, he produces fear, murder and wonder (vs. 18).

5.   "Yes" … "Maybe" … "No" — Has Jesus' insistence pushed you out of the "Maybe" slot? On which side have you landed?

12 The next day as they were leaving Bethany, Jesus was hungry. 13 Seeing in the distance a fig tree in leaf, he went to find out if it had any fruit. When he reached it, he found nothing but leaves, because it was not the season for figs. 14 Then he said to the tree, "May no one ever eat fruit from you again." And his disciples heard him say it. 15 On reaching Jerusalem, Jesus entered the temple area and began driving out those who were buying and selling there. He overturned the tables of the money changers and the benches of those selling doves, 16 and would not allow anyone to carry merchandise through the temple courts. 17 And as he taught them, he said, "Is it not written: "'My house will be called a house of prayer for all nations'? But you have made it 'a den of robbers.'" 18 The chief priests and the teachers of the law heard this and began looking for a way to kill him, for they feared him, because the whole crowd was amazed at his teaching. 19 When evening came, they went out of the city. 20 In the morning, as they went along, they saw the fig tree withered from the roots. 21 Peter remembered and said to Jesus, "Rabbi, look! The fig tree you cursed has withered!" 22 "Have faith in God," Jesus answered. 23 "I tell you the truth, if anyone says to this mountain, 'Go, throw yourself into the sea,' and does not doubt in his heart but believes that what he says will happen, it will be done for him. 24 Therefore I tell you, whatever you ask for in prayer, believe that you have received it, and it will be yours. 25 And when you stand praying, if you hold anything against anyone, forgive him, so that your Father in heaven may forgive you your sins."

My Thoughts Today …

Read Mark 11:27-33

Jesus is traveling daily to Jerusalem to teach in the temple. This is a dangerous habit. After all, his presumptuous purging of the temple has just given more fuel to the hatred that is building against him. It is a hostility that will not rest until he is killed. So, it is not surprising that those in charge demand to see his credentials.

"By What Authority" (vs. 28) — This question is carefully framed to be a forced dilemma. Any answer is a blind alley leading Jesus into the hands of his opposition:

· If he claims Human Authority, his own or some other, he can be arrested for treason, incompetence or both.

· If he claims God's Authority, he can be arrested for blasphemy.

Clearly the motive behind their question is devious. But in spite of their motive, the question raises the central issue in every human life — what is the Authority, Purpose and Meaning for what we do?

1. If you had recognized the motive behind this question, would you have answered? Why or why not?

2. How difficult is it for you to identify and describe the principal authority of your life?

3. Take a minute and write down a description of that authority.

"Answer Me And I Will Answer You" (vs. 29) — Seeing the trap of the religious leaders Jesus replies, as he has done before (2:9,19, 25ff; 3:4, 23; 10:3), with a more difficult counter-dilemma. He reminds them of John the Baptist's preaching of repentance and then asks, "Who authorized his ministry?" Now, they have their own forced dilemma to answer.

· If they say that John's baptism is from God Jesus will then ask them why they opposed it. Both know that if the temple leaders had accepted John, they would be able to accept Jesus (1:2, 7-8).

· Once again fear is the ruling emotion here (vs. 32; cf. vs. 18). It prevents an honest answer. And by refusing to answer, the religious leaders show the frailty of their base of authority.

4. When you face popular opinion, what usually comes to the surface — faith or fear?

5. Where does "peer pressure" get its power and influence?

"Neither Will I Tell You" (vs. 33) — Jesus is not trying to evade the issue because he is afraid. He knows that his enemies are only pretending that they want to know more about his credentials. He also knows that the best way to answer is by allowing or, in this case, forcing his opponents to come to the conclusion themselves. In doing so, he not only faces squarely the authority issue, but he also forces his opponents to live under it.

6. Why are so many people afraid to know the truth about themselves?

7. What usually follows a refusal to face the truth?

27 They arrived again in Jerusalem, and while Jesus was walking in the temple courts, the chief priests, the teachers of the law and the elders came to him. 28 "By what authority are you doing these things?" they asked. "And who gave you authority to do this?" 29 Jesus replied, "I will ask you one question. Answer me, and I will tell you by what authority I am doing these things. 30 John's baptism—was it from heaven, or from men? Tell me!" 31 They discussed it among themselves and said, "If we say, 'From heaven,' he will ask, 'Then why didn't you believe him?' 32 But if we say, 'From men' . . . ." (They feared the people, for everyone held that John really was a prophet.) 33 So they answered Jesus, "We don't know." Jesus said, "Neither will I tell you by what authority I am doing these things."

My Thoughts Today ...

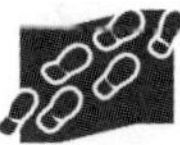

Read Mark 12:1-12

Building on his latest victory, Jesus tells a striking parable designed to confront and accuse the religious authorities (vs. 1, 12). Most of his parables focus on a single theme — the kingdom of God. They describe its power, purpose and reception.

Until now, the parables have been primarily aimed at the curious, the interested, the seeker. Until his entry into Jerusalem Jesus has rarely initiated a discussion with his enemies. But now, confrontation becomes an unavoidable part of his mission. Here he faces the foot soldiers in this evil battle. But, eventually he will have to confront the very source of the evil that opposes him — "The prince of this world" (Jn 14:30).

1.   Why is confrontation in Jesus' ministry just as valid as compassion?

2.   Why is it difficult for some of us to picture Jesus in conflict?

After refusing to answer any questions about his authority in the last episode (11:27-33), Jesus now fully answers by claiming divine authority. But, true to form, he conceals his answer in a simple parable with a thinly veiled meaning. The temple authorities are unable to arrest him or even accuse him of wrong. After all, how can they object to a simple story? But what a story:

Unrequited Love — In his "simple" story the vineyard is Israel. God, the owner, has sent one messenger after another to meet with those entrusted with his vineyard. But every messenger has encountered rejection and mistreatment from the farmers ruling the nation. Finally, in a great climax of ignored love, God sends his own son. They kill him. This is a story of God's generosity, trust, patience and pain.

3.   Is God thought of more in terms of love or wrath? Why?

4.   What has God "entrusted" to you?

5.   Have you been trustworthy? Why or why not?

6.   Why has God been so patient with the human race?

Rejected Stone — Jesus' description of the son as one "whom he loved" (vs. 6) clearly echoes a message repeatedly given to him by God (1:11; 9:7). It is this deep sense of love that enables him to walk into this city of enemies. He regards himself as a "Son" who brings God's final message (cf. Heb 1:1-2). This is a story of Jesus' commitment to his Father's mission.

7.   How can love heal the wounds of rejection?

8.   How did God's love empower Jesus to continue his mission?

The Final Chapter — This parable describes the end of one chapter in human history and the beginning of another. After all, the owner has no alternative except to end his contract with the farmers and give the vineyard to other tenants (vs. 9). The lesson is clear. To refuse privileges and responsibilities is to pass them on to someone else. This story looks forward to the new tenant — the church.

9.   What does apathy do to the Christian mission?

10.   How is the church today vulnerable to the same mistakes that Israel made?

1 He then began to speak to them in parables: "A man planted a vineyard. He put a wall around it, dug a pit for the winepress and built a watchtower. Then he rented the vineyard to some farmers and went away on a journey. 2 At harvest time he sent a servant to the tenants to collect from them some of the fruit of the vineyard. 3 But they seized him, beat him and sent him away empty-handed. 4 Then he sent another servant to them; they struck this man on the head and treated him shamefully. 5 He sent still another, and that one they killed. He sent many others; some of them they beat, others they killed. 6 "He had one left to send, a son, whom he loved. He sent him last of all, saying, 'They will respect my son.' 7 "But the tenants said to one another, 'This is the heir. Come, let's kill him, and the inheritance will be ours.' 8 So they took him and killed him, and threw him out of the vineyard. 9 "What then will the owner of the vineyard do? He will come and kill those tenants and give the vineyard to others. 10 Haven't you read this scripture: "'The stone the builders rejected has become the capstone; 11 the Lord has done this, and it is marvelous in our eyes'?" 12 Then they looked for a way to arrest him because they knew he had spoken the parable against them. But they were afraid of the crowd; so they left him and went away.

My Thoughts Today …

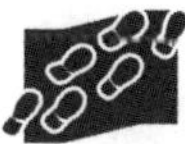

Read Mark 12:13-17

For the last 23 years Judea has been under direct Roman rule. Its government is led by a Roman military procurator, and is enforced by Roman troops. Every Jew living directly under this Roman rule must pay the Roman tribute with a silver denarii. This coin is decorated with the name and picture of the Emperor Tiberius. This intentional collision of uncomfortable ideas and loyalties is the background behind the question now brought to Jesus.

Self Incrimination — Jesus repeatedly defeats and exposes his religious enemies as they try to "catch him in his words" (vs. 13). But for the leaders of the religious establishment this is much more than a battle of words. They want Jesus dead (11:18). In fact, they have been plotting his death for a long time (3:6). But first they must publicly discredit him (cf. 11:18, 32; 12:12) and they make their attempt with the most dangerous political and religious question of the day— Taxes. They know that any answer Jesus can give will show him to be disloyal to someone. It doesn't really matter to them if he is discredited in the eyes of the people for siding with the Herodians or if he conflicts with the Roman authorities for opposing taxes. They just want him stopped.

1.   **When attacked, openly or deceitfully, how do you usually respond?**

2.   **How do you feel when you have to disappoint someone?**

Unnatural Alliance —The Herodians and Pharisees are religious and political enemies and it is ironic to see how they have put aside their own differences in order to consolidate their attack. Mutual hate unifies them in an effort to destroy Jesus.

3.   **Why is public opinion so important to religious leaders today?**

4.   **Why was it not as important to Jesus?**

5.   **After refusing to answer direct questions (11:27-33), why does Jesus now respond to such an underhanded question?**

Clashing Pictures — Jesus refuses to play their game by taking their superficial question to a deeper, more uncomfortable level. He makes them pull the denarii out of their own pockets, showing that this is their problem as well as his. Besides, they have oversimplified the whole question. Without intending to, they have raised the most important issue of all (vs. 17):

· Give To Caesar What Is Caesar's — When the denarii is produced, Jesus points to the picture stamped on it to demonstrate that the coin belongs to Caesar.

· Give To God What Is God's — Then, with an implied question, Jesus asks whose picture is stamped on every human life. This is a powerful challenge to Jews who believe they are made in God's image. The Pharisees and Herodians are speechless because their own lives are out of harmony with the one whose image they wear.

6.   **What superficial concerns (like taxes) do we have today?**

7.   **Why do we sometimes avoid the real issue of life?**

8.   **If you took Jesus' words seriously and gave "to God what is God's" what would have to change in your life?**

Mark 12:13-17

13 Later they sent some of the Pharisees and Herodians to Jesus to catch him in his words. 14 They came to him and said, "Teacher, we know you are a man of integrity. You aren't swayed by men, because you pay no attention to who they are; but you teach the way of God in accordance with the truth. Is it right to pay taxes to Caesar or not? 15 Should we pay or shouldn't we?" But Jesus knew their hypocrisy. "Why are you trying to trap me?" he asked. "Bring me a denarius and let me look at it." 16 They brought the coin, and he asked them, "Whose portrait is this? And whose inscription?" "Caesar's," they replied. 17 Then Jesus said to them, "Give to Caesar what is Caesar's and to God what is God's." And they were amazed at him.

My Thoughts Today …

Read Mark 12:18-27

This is the only time Mark mentions the Sadducees. But still they play a major role in the final days of Jesus' life. He is well inside their territory and he knows that, as the aristocracy of the city, they are always well informed and very much in control.

Their Origin — The history of the Sadducees is unclear. It is possible that they come from the Zadokites, a family of High-priests in the days of David and Solomon (2 Sa 8:17; 15:24; 20:25). But while their history is uncertain, their control of Jerusalem is not.

Their Power — The Sadducees belong to the leading families of Jerusalem. From these families the high priests are appointed. They stay in power through compromise, bribery and violence. They are wealthy, well educated, worldly and uncomfortable with Jesus' popularity.

1.   **What is it about power that easily corrupts religion?**

2.   **How does Jesus, with all his power, remain true to his mission?**

3.   **What is the process that turns a faithful heart into a hard heart?**

Unlike the Pharisees, the Sadducees reject oral tradition and hold only to the five books of Moses. Their denial of the resurrection (cf. Ac 23:7-8) has long been the center of their dispute with the Pharisees. Now they bring the issue to Jesus:

"The Man Must Marry The Widow" (vs. 19) — The story they bring is an outlandishly overtold application of the Levirate Law. This title comes from the Latin term Levir, which means brother-in-law. This law is designed to perpetuate the family line of a man who dies childless (Dt 25:5-10). It is clear that they bring it as a trap question, intended to ridicule Jesus and the whole idea of resurrection. It is impressive that, even though the Sadducees are not seriously seeking a solution, Jesus doesn't reject their story as unreasonable. Instead, he meets them on their own ground and even answers them from a part of the Bible they can accept (Ex 3:6).

4.   **What is the difference between an honest seeker and a deceitful schemer?**

5.   **Why did Jesus even reply?**

"You Do Not Know" (vs. 24) — In Exodus 3 God presents himself to Moses as the God of Patriarchs who had died years before. But he speaks of them in the present tense — "I am." He is still their God because they exist in a resurrected life. Either the Sadducees had never considered this or they chose to ignore it!

6.   **How can one spend years reading a text and still miss its meaning?**

7.   **Why does humility continue to seek, to learn and to change?**

"You Are Badly Mistaken" (vs. 27) — The Sadducees are ignorant of what living forever with God can mean even for their present life. They are amassing worldly power and sinking their roots into this Earthly life. But they are missing the "power of God" (vs. 24) and the strength of Eternal life.

8.   **How does the promise of resurrection bring power to our lives?**

Mark 12:18-27

18 Then the Sadducees, who say there is no resurrection, came to him with a question. 19 "Teacher," they said, "Moses wrote for us that if a man's brother dies and leaves a wife but no children, the man must marry the widow and have children for his brother. 20 Now there were seven brothers. The first one married and died without leaving any children. 21 The second one married the widow, but he also died, leaving no child. It was the same with the third. 22 In fact, none of the seven left any children. Last of all, the woman died too. 23 At the resurrection whose wife will she be, since the seven were married to her?" 24 Jesus replied, "Are you not in error because you do not know the Scriptures or the power of God? 25 When the dead rise, they will neither marry nor be given in marriage; they will be like the angels in heaven. 26 Now about the dead rising—have you not read in the book of Moses, in the account of the bush, how God said to him, 'I am the God of Abraham, the God of Isaac, and the God of Jacob'? 27 He is not the God of the dead, but of the living. You are badly mistaken!"

My Thoughts Today ...

Read Mark 12:28-34

After a frustrating encounter with critics, Jesus now meets one who is "not far from the kingdom of God" (vs. 34). This scribe asks a question that touches the very heart of Jesus' purpose. His question had often been a matter of debate among rabbis who were trying to find the essence of the law or who were trying to prioritize the 613 commandments. Several statements in the Old Testament were offered as the essence of the law:

Psalm 15	**Isaiah 33:15**	**Isaiah 66:2**
Blameless walk, true heart	Walks righteously	A humble heart
Does neighbor no wrong	Speaks the truth	A contrite spirit
Despises evil, keeps word	Refuses extorted gain	Respects the word
Honest deeds and tongue	Refuses bribes	
Does not slur fellowman	Refuses to hear murder plots	**Micah 6:8**
Honors those who fear God	Will not consider evil	To act justly
Keeps his oath, generous		To love mercy
Does not exploit innocent	**Habakkuk 2:4**	To walk humbly
	Living by faith	

Jesus answers with two quotations (Dt 6:4ff; Lev 19:18). He interprets every relationship, God to man and man to man, with the single word "Love."

"The Most Important One" (vs. 29) — The first Hebrew word in Deuteronomy 6:4 is Shema, which means "hear." The word Shema came to be used as the title for the entire statement of faith, which pious Jews recite three times daily:

Hear, O Israel: The Lord our God, the Lord is one.
Love the Lord your God with all your heart and with all your soul and with all your strength.

1.   What does it mean to love God with our heart, soul, mind and strength?

2.   What are other competing world-views?

"More Important Than Sacrifice" (vs. 33) — An old warning against hypocrisy echoes through this conversation (1 Sa 15:22; Ps 40:6; 51:16; Hos 6:6). Jesus himself is replacing the temple as the place where God is met.

· 11:1-11 — Jesus enters the city going immediately to the temple.

· 11:12-26 — Jesus causes the temple disturbance.

· 11:27; 12:35, 41 — Jesus clashes with the temple leadership.

· 13:1-2 — Jesus predicts the temple's destruction (cf. 14:58 Jn 2:19)

· 15:38 — At Jesus' death, the curtain of the temple is ripped in two.

3.   Why is Jesus himself the clearest picture of God (cf. Heb 1:1-3)?

"Not Far From The Kingdom" (vs. 34) — This man is near, but has not yet arrived. He agrees with Jesus. But here it stops. He is a hearer, but not a doer.

4.   How can a person move from hearing to doing?

5.   How can thoughts and attitudes keep a person "stuck" as only a hearer?

28 One of the teachers of the law came and heard them debating. Noticing that Jesus had given them a good answer, he asked him, "Of all the commandments, which is the most important?" 29 "The most important one," answered Jesus, "is this: 'Hear, O Israel, the Lord our God, the Lord is one. 30 Love the Lord your God with all your heart and with all your soul and with all your mind and with all your strength.' 31 The second is this: 'Love your neighbor as yourself.' There is no commandment greater than these." 32 "Well said, teacher," the man replied. "You are right in saying that God is one and there is no other but him. 33 To love him with all your heart, with all your understanding and with all your strength, and to love your neighbor as yourself is more important than all burnt offerings and sacrifices." 34 When Jesus saw that he had answered wisely, he said to him, "You are not far from the kingdom of God." And from then on no one dared ask him any more questions

My Thoughts Today ...

Read Mark 12:35-37

Jesus has been the target for days. Questions have been shot from all sides. Genuine seekers have taken aim at his heart, looking for real answers. But, uncomfortable critics have simply gone for the "jugular" looking for a kill.

1. How does Jesus separate the genuine seeker from the critic?

2. How has his response to each differed?

Jesus has been moving through several days of controversial questions. Time after time someone else has taken the initiative and raised a difficult question. But now, Jesus steps into the role of initiator and asks a question of his own.

Question (vs. 35) — Jesus is a master at answering questions. But he is even better at asking them. For some time he has avoided the issue of his identity. He first raised it with the apostles (8:27-30). But now, he raises it with a wider audience. His question shows that to define Messiah as David's descendant is true but inadequate. David is pictured as a heroic king and several Old Testament prophets promise another king who will come as David's descendant to rule with the same devotion and success (Isa 9:6-7; 16:5; Jer 23:5; 30:8-9; Eze 34:23-24; 37:24; Hos. 3:5; Am 9:11). In Jesus day, this hope for another David has grown into a fiercely patriotic expectation. This is why Jesus now intentionally confronts this twisted picture.

3. How has Jesus gradually opened the subject of his identity?

4. After avoiding the topic earlier, why does he intentionally open a discussion with the teachers of the Law now?

Quotation (vs. 36) — In their wait for the Messiah, generations of scribes had focused on genealogies of the house of David. It was a flawed tunnel vision that fed their own political interests. They looked for the Son of David, but not the Lord of David. The quotation from Psalm 110 does not mean that the Messiah cannot be David's son, but that the Messiah cannot merely be David's son. He is much more. Later, the resurrected Jesus will say through the apostle John:

> *I, Jesus, have sent my angel to give you this testimony for the churches.*
> *I am the Root and the Offspring of David,*
> *and the bright Morning Star.*
> *Revelation 22:16*

5. Psalm 110 was always there, but they missed it. Why? How?

6. There are many ancient facts about Jesus that have always been true. Reflect on one or two that have recently become "new" to you.

Quandary (vs. 37) — Don't forget about the crowd. They are always there. Sometimes they are silent and puzzled. At other times they are gasping with astonishment. Here they are laughing with satisfied delight. But, as they watch Jesus take the offensive and move deeper into the city, do they see his ultimate destiny? Do they see his final appointment with the cross?

7. His deliberate trek into the city brings salvation — your salvation. Thank him!

35 While Jesus was teaching in the temple courts, he asked, "How is it that the teachers of the law say that the Christ is the son of David? 36 David himself, speaking by the Holy Spirit, declared: 'The Lord said to my Lord: "Sit at my right hand until I put your enemies under your feet."' 37 David himself calls him 'Lord.' How then can he be his son?" The large crowd listened to him with delight.

My Thoughts Today ...

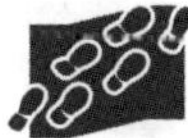

What I Learned This Week ...

... About Jesus

... About Ministry

... About Myself

Day 64
12:38-40

Day 65
12:41-44

Day 66
13:1-2

Day 67
13:3-8

Day 68
13:9-13

Week 10   The Temple
Day 64-70   Mark 12:38-13:31

Day 69
13:14-23

Day 70
13:24-31

The Temple

Mark 12:38-13:31

This week, as you walk with Jesus, you will see him in the Temple contrasting the corrupt religion of the wealthy high-born with the sacrificial religion of the faithful widows. Watch him prepare his followers for the hardships ahead. Listen to him picture the devastation of the Temple, the city of Jerusalem, and the end of the world.

Use the time to measure your own faith.

My Prayer For This Week …

Read Mark 12:38-40

There is no break in Jesus' stride. Months of patient preparation and calculated waiting now give way to uninhibited honesty. After talking with the teachers of the law, Jesus now turns and talks about them. After commenting on their teaching (vs. 35-37), he turns to their practice (vs. 38-40). After all, the two are inseparable. Belief affects action and action influences belief.

1. Why are belief and action so inseparable?

2. With is easier for you — to talk with or about someone? Why?

The role of the Scribe has a long history (2 Sa 8:17; 2 Ki 18:18; Jer 8:8). Along their journey, they have found a prominent place as teachers, magistrates and consultants. But Jesus looks much deeper and finds much more. In their rise to power, the Scribes have developed certain desires that look very respectable on the outside. But Jesus peels back the surface.

They Want To Be Known — The long robe reaching almost to the floor is worn by the scribe during times of prayer or while performing other scribal duties. It is an outward sign of their devotion to God. But with carefully planned trips through the city streets, it can also be a sign of their devotion to themselves.

3. How can we call attention to our faith and our God, but not to ourselves (cf. Mt 5:14-16)?

They Want To Be Important — The chief seats in the synagogue are up front facing the congregation. In this way, the teachers of the law can see everyone there. But more importantly, they can be seen by everyone there. This is really what they want — to have a prominent place and to be thought of as an important person.

4. How can we remain humble when God honors us with leadership?

They Want To Be Honored — It is a short step from wanting special treatment to demanding it. And with self in the spotlight, others are easily forgotten. Jesus' brother James put it this way:

> *Suppose a man comes into your meeting wearing a gold ring and fine clothes,*
> *and a poor man in shabby clothes also comes in.*
> *If you show special attention to the man wearing fine clothes and say,*
> *"Here's a good seat for you,"*
> *but say to the poor man, "You stand there" or "Sit on the floor by my feet,"*
> *have you not discriminated among yourselves and become judges with evil thoughts?*
> *James 2:2-4*

5. How can honor lead to and nurture humility?

They Want To Be Respected — Scribes would often serve as consultants in estate planning for widows. And there is no better way to gain the respect of a lonely, grieving widow than with a show of pious spirituality. But, it also guarantees a generous consulting fee.

6. Who are the people in our society today who, like the widows in Jesus' day, are vulnerable to religious exploitation? Who is doing the exploiting today?

7. How can those in "helping" roles protect themselves from greed?

38 As he taught, Jesus said, Watch out for the teachers of the law. They like to walk around in flowing robes and be greeted in the marketplaces, 39 and have the most important seats in the synagogues and the places of honor at banquets. 40 They devour widows' houses and for a show make lengthy prayers. Such men will be punished most severely.

My Thoughts Today ...

Read Mark 12:41-44

As Jesus moves from one part of the temple to another, he also moves from a story of pride to a story of humility. He makes several sharp contrasts between: the upper class and the lower class, the rich and the poor, external religion and internal religion.

Jesus leaves the place where he has been teaching, and finds an out of the way place in the Court of Women where he can sit and watch.

1.   How would you feel if God found a place in your worship service to sit and watch?

2.   How would it affect your posture, your singing or your attentiveness?

According to ancient Jewish tradition, lining the walls of the Court of Women are thirteen trumpet-shaped receptacles (Mishna, Shekalim 6:5). These are used to collect the gifts of the worshipers. They are carefully placed in the Court of Women rather than deeper in the Temple because this court is the innermost point to which women are allowed to go. It seems ironic that even though only a few can penetrate the deepest and holiest places of the Temple, great care is taken to make the collection containers available to everyone.

3.   Why have economics often been a stumbling block for religion and for religious leaders?

"Jesus Sat Down" (vs. 41) — This is a time for observation and study. And so, Jesus studies the people. But he looks much deeper than the typical "Mall-Watcher" of today. He looks beyond the "flowing robes" (vs. 38) and sees into the heart.

4.   Why is the heart the real source of wealth and riches?

5.   How and why are outward appearances usually misleading?

"Many Rich People" (vs. 41) — The Bible never condemns riches or simply being wealthy, but it does give very strict warnings concerning the dangers of wealth.

> *For the love of money is a root of all kinds of evil.*
> *Some people, eager for money, have wandered from the faith and pierced themselves with many griefs.*
> *1 Timothy 6:10*

"A Poor Widow" (vs. 42) — This widow has no social standing. Probably no one else is studying her as Jesus is, but if someone else is watching they will probably judge her gift as worthless. She offers only two copper coins and even they are the smallest coins in circulation.

6.   But, what has poverty taught this widow about giving?

7.   What do you see in her heart?

"Calling His Disciples" (vs. 43) — Jesus has often called his disciples together to learn a lesson from some experience in daily life (3:13; 6:7; 8:1, 34; 10:42). Here he teaches that the best measure of commitment is found not in what is given, but in what is kept. The contrast with the preceding story of the scribe who wanted to be known, honored and respected is unmistakable. While some "devour widow's houses" (vs. 40), the widows are giving all that they have.

8.   Some "give out of their wealth" while others "give out of their poverty." What is the difference?

41 Jesus sat down opposite the place where the offerings were put and watched the crowd putting their money into the temple treasury. Many rich people threw in large amounts. 42 But a poor widow came and put in two very small copper coins, worth only a fraction of a penny. 43 Calling his disciples to him, Jesus said, "I tell you the truth, this poor widow has put more into the treasury than all the others. 44 They all gave out of their wealth; but she, out of her poverty, put in everything — all she had to live on."

My Thoughts Today …

Read Mark 13:1-2

All this time Jesus has been in the temple. It is the center-piece of Jewish religion. But only those living nearby have the opportunity to see the temple on a somewhat frequent basis. For Jesus and his small band of followers it is an awesome experience. To walk through the temple and hear their leader teach and amaze the crowds must fill the disciples with great pride.

1.   Why does pride so easily emerge as our favorite leaders impress and win?

2.   How do you feel when your spiritual champions fail to win the approval of others?

They are full of pride … but not for long. This place of worship is rapidly becoming a place of conflict, envy, slander and carefully laid traps. Again and again Jesus faces and defeats his religious enemies. But finally, he has had enough. Finally, he is ready to leave.

3.   As the Twelve walk with Jesus through the beautiful courts and follow him through the massive temple doors to the outside, imagine their thoughts.

The Disciples — Herod's temple was under construction for 46 years (Jn 2:20). It rose 200 feet above Jerusalem and cast a sparkling image from its marble walls and golden dome. Some stones weighed 100 tons each. The historian Josephus (Ant 15.11.3) reports that the stones were 37 feet long, 18 feet wide, and 12 feet high. How could something so huge and so solid, appearing to be so permanent feel so spiritually empty? Jesus had exposed the religious establishment. Imagine the impact of his parting words (Lk 13:35):

Look, your house is left to you desolate.

The disciples are again confused and searching for words. They cannot believe that one of the architectural wonders of the world has lost its magnificence. And so, they do what many of us do when we feel unhappy and uncertain. They begin to focus on the outside. They look for an answer to their sadness in the appearance and size of the temple.

4.   When faced with our religious failures, why do we fall back on our own viewpoints rather than continue to trust and seek God's?

Jesus — Echoing the ancient prophets (Mic 3:12; Jer 27:6, 18) Jesus makes it very clear that holiness is not a matter of structure — in a temple or in a life. God must still be present. Jesus holds out no hope for the temple. Forty years later, Jerusalem will be taken by Titus, the son of the emperor Vespasian. The eyewitness Josephus will estimate that over one million Jews, crowded together in the city, will die. Listen to his report (Wars 7.1-3)

The emperor ordered the entire city and sanctuary to be razed to the ground,
except only the highest towers, Phasael, Hippicus, and Mariamne . . .
All the rest . . . was so completely razed to the ground
as to leave future visitors to the spot no reason to believe
that it had ever been inhabited.

5.   Why do size and appearances have such power over us?

6.   Why do we trust in human traditions and achievements?

1 As he was leaving the temple, one of his disciples said to him, "Look, Teacher! What massive stones! What magnificent buildings!" 2 "Do you see all these great buildings?" replied Jesus. "Not one stone here will be left on another; every one will be thrown down."

My Thoughts Today …

Read Mark 13:3-8

In response to Jesus' announcement that the temple will be destroyed, it is not surprising that four of the disciples want to know more (vs. 3). Notice especially the personal pronouns in this chapter:

"us" — (vs. 4)   "them" — (vs. 5)   "you" — (vs. 5, 7, 9, 11, 13)

This is first and foremost a conversation with the disciples named here. Also notice that in response to their very specific questions about when and what, Jesus does not give either a date or a specific sign to use to determine the date. In fact, the answer Jesus begins to give, shifts the focus away from the panic of how and when and concentrates instead on being careful, cautious and ready at all times.

1.   Why do reports of "wars" "earthquakes" and " famine" often send people into a religious panic?

Jesus seems to anticipate this potential panic, so he deliberately introduces three kinds of trauma common to every generation:

Religious Extremism (vs. 5-6) — There will always be those who claim special religious knowledge and insight. Jesus says these "Christ-figures" will come saying "I am he." In the original language he means they are using the title "I Am," one of the divine names (cf. Jn 18:5). Jesus is saying be very careful whom you follow.

2.   How have you encountered religious extremism?

3.   Where do you see it? What are the claims that are made today?

Social Turbulence (vs. 7-8) — As long as people share life on planet earth they will be fighting each other. There will always be national and international conflict. And while the wars and rumors of wars are reason to stop and think, Jesus says keep your head clear and looking forward.

4.   What is the social turbulence in our own time and experience?

5.   How does it shape the religious views of our day?

Natural Disaster (vs. 8) — There was a famine in Judea in AD 46. There were earthquakes in Pompeii and Laodicea in AD 61-62. When Krakatoa erupted in 1883, it killed 36,000 people and could be heard for 3,000 miles. These and countless other natural disasters are a regular part of the march of time, but not necessarily a sign of the end of time.

6.   Why do religious people often see these kinds of traumas as unique to their own time and place?

7.   Why is fear so easily triggered?

Since these are common in every generation and in every age, Jesus warns his disciples not to see these events as signs of final judgment. Instead, he says "do not be alarmed" (vs. 7). To let the regular breakdown of human and natural history determine our reaction is to give in to panic.

8.   How does this shape our theology?

9.   What does this do to our mission?

3 As Jesus was sitting on the Mount of Olives opposite the temple, Peter, James, John and Andrew asked him privately, 4 "Tell us, when will these things happen? And what will be the sign that they are all about to be fulfilled?" 5 Jesus said to them: "Watch out that no one deceives you. 6 Many will come in my name, claiming, 'I am he,' and will deceive many. 7 When you hear of wars and rumors of wars, do not be alarmed. Such things must happen, but the end is still to come. 8 Nation will rise against nation, and kingdom against kingdom. There will be earthquakes in various places, and famines. These are the beginning of birth pains.

My Thoughts Today ...

Read Mark 13:9-13

Six times in this chapter, Jesus warns his disciples to be watchful and to stay on their guard (vs. 5, 9, 23, 33, 35, 37). After being very clear about his own suffering, he leaves no doubt that to choose him is to choose a hard way. In fact, in verse 9 he predicts three major occasions of suffering for his followers:

"Local Councils" …

> *Having brought the apostles, they made them appear before The Sanhedrin....*
> *They called the apostles in and had them flogged.*
> *Then they ordered them not to speak in the name of Jesus, and let them go.*
> *The apostles left the Sanhedrin, rejoicing*
> *because they had been counted worthy of suffering disgrace for the Name.*
> *Acts 5:27, 40-41*

"Governors" …

> *They brought their charges against Paul before The Governor.*
> *When Paul was called in, Tertullus presented his case before Felix . . .*
> *When two years had passed, Felix was succeeded by Porcius Festus,*
> *but because Felix wanted to grant a favor to the Jews, he left Paul in prison.*
> *Acts 24:1-2, 27*

"Kings" …

> *The next day Agrippa and Bernice came with great pomp*
> *and entered the audience room with the high ranking officer*
> *and the leading men of the city.*
> *At the command of Festus, Paul was brought in.*
> *Festus said: "King Agrippa, and all who are present with us, you see this man!*
> *The whole Jewish community has petitioned me about him in Jerusalem*
> *and here is Caesarea, shouting that he ought not to live any longer"*
> *Acts 25:23-24*

All of Jesus' predictions occurred just as he said. But why did these early Christians attract this kind of persecution and suffering? One sentence makes it all perfectly clear:

> *When they saw the courage of Peter and John*
> *and realized that they were unschooled, ordinary men,*
> *they were astonished and they took note that these men had been With Jesus*
> *Acts 4:13*

These early Christians learned about the authority of suffering from Jesus.

1. **Have you ever know someone who suffered for their faith?**

2. **What is the best way to prepare yourself for religious suffering?**

3. **What is difference between religious suffering then and now?**

4. **How were Jesus' disciples supposed to act when they were arrested for their faith?**

9 "You must be on your guard. You will be handed over to the local councils and flogged in the synagogues. On account of me you will stand before governors and kings as witnesses to them. 10 And the gospel must first be preached to all nations. 11 Whenever you are arrested and brought to trial, do not worry beforehand about what to say. Just say whatever is given you at the time, for it is not you speaking, but the Holy Spirit. 12 "Brother will betray brother to death, and a father his child. Children will rebel against their parents and have them put to death. 13 All men will hate you because of me, but he who stands firm to the end will be saved.

My Thoughts Today …

Read Mark 13:14-23

Having predicted the difficulties that the disciples would be facing in their future ministry, Jesus now describes a coming event that is so horrible that he reaches back to the book of Daniel for his words. He calls it "the abomination that causes desolation" (vs. 14). This phrase from Daniel (9:27; 11:31; 21:11) comes from a section rich in vivid symbolism. It is characteristic of the visions recorded in the last part of Daniel's writing. In later centuries it became a Jewish code phrase used to describe horrible religious atrocities.

168 BC — The hated Syrian ruler Antiochus Epiphanes sacrificed a pig to Zeus on the temple altar (1 Macc 1:54). He also set up places of prostitution in the outer courts and banned Judaism.

AD 40 — The Roman emperor Caligula attempted to set up his own statue in the temple on the altar of burnt offerings (Josephus, Jewish War, 2.10.1).

But the abomination that Jesus is probably describing is the threat of desecration posed by the later gathering of Roman armies around the city.

When you see Jerusalem surrounded by armies, you will know that its desolation is near.
Luke 21:20

AD 67-68 — It will be during the siege of Jerusalem that the abomination will become even more horrible. And sadly, it will come from the Jewish community itself. Josephus will report that during the siege several rival Jewish groups will fight inside the city. Jewish Zealots will eventually occupy the temple during AD 67-68. They will pile up their murdered Jewish brothers in the Holy of Holies. These acts of abomination will culminate in the ritual farce of installing a clown named Phanni as the chief priest of the temple.

1.   As a Christian trapped in Jerusalem how would you survive?

2.   What would you pray about?

3.   How important would a Christian community be?

Jesus warns that there will be no time and no relief. To hesitate is to die. And true to his prediction, almost 100,000 Jews will be captured and more than 1,000,000 will die of starvation and violence. But the historian Eusebius reports that many Christians remembering Jesus' words will quickly flee to Pella in Perea east of the Jordan in the Transjordan area (Ecclesiastical History, 3.5.3). To leave so quickly, they will have to overcome several obstacles:

Possessions (vs. 15-16) — Personal items, household articles, "a coat in the field." Nothing should stand in the way of immediate escape.

Family Duties (vs. 17) — Pregnant women, nursing mothers and everyone with children or a family will be even more hard pressed to find safety quickly.

Nature (vs. 18) — Winter flooding, washed out roads and bridges. Being on the move without the usual stored collection of food and supplies will further increase the difficulty of survival.

False Hope (vs. 21-22) — Many will take advantage of the widespread panic and disorganization to proclaim themselves as the answer. Public pressure to follow false saviors will be widespread.

4.   In the above list, which obstacle would be the most difficult for you? Why?

14 "When you see 'the abomination that causes desolation' standing where it does not belong — let the reader understand — then let those who are in Judea flee to the mountains. 15 Let no one on the roof of his house go down or enter the house to take anything out. 16 Let no one in the field go back to get his cloak. 17 How dreadful it will be in those days for pregnant women and nursing mothers! 18 Pray that this will not take place in winter, 19 because those will be days of distress unequaled from the beginning, when God created the world, until now — and never to be equaled again. 20 If the Lord had not cut short those days, no one would survive. But for the sake of the elect, whom he has chosen, he has shortened them. 21 At that time if anyone says to you, 'Look, here is the Christ!' or, 'Look, there he is!' do not believe it. 22 For false Christs and false prophets will appear and perform signs and miracles to deceive the elect — if that were possible. 23 So be on your guard; I have told you everything ahead of time.

My Thoughts Today …

Read Mark 13:24-31

Understanding the structure of this chapter is similar to driving across a great plain toward a huge range of mountains. At first, the mountains appear to be a single unit because, from a distance, they can all be seen at one time. But, as the distance closes, it becomes clear that while some mountain peaks are much closer, others are very far away.

In this section Jesus changes his language. It becomes cosmic and reaches far into the future. He leaves, for a moment, his discussion of the destruction of Jerusalem and looks at the end of time.

Change Of Pronouns — Up until now Jesus has consistently directed his words of warning to the disciples. He affirms that the events he is describing will be a part of their own personal experience. They ask "tell us" (vs. 4). He answers "to them" (vs. 5). And he consistently uses the personal pronoun "you" (vs. 5, 7, 9, 11, 13, 14, 21, 23, 28, 29, 30, 33, 35, 36, 37). In only this one section (vs. 24-27) does he drop his use of the pronoun "you."

Vivid Language — Jesus ceases his previous description of "natural" disasters (earthquakes, famine etc.). Here he describes "unnatural" disasters (darkening sun and moon, stars deviating from their orbits, shaking of the heavens). These all lie outside any possible human prediction or explanation.

1.   Why does Jesus move from discussing the end of Jerusalem to discussing the end of the world?

After warning of the false Christs, Jesus points to the end of time and the coming of the true Messiah. He is clear that, when the Messiah comes, he will:

Come In The Clouds — The clouds were an age old signal of God's presence (Ex 16:10; 19:9; 24:15-16; 33:9; Lev 16:2; Nu 11:25; 1 Ki 8:10). Earlier in this story, at the Transfiguration, God made his presence known with a cloud:

> *Then a cloud appeared and enveloped them, and a voice came from the cloud:*
> *"This is my Son, whom I love.*
> *Listen to him!"*
> *Mark 9:7*

Gather The Elect — He will gather them from every direction. The "four winds" describe the four points on a compass (cf. Isa 11:12; Zec 2:6). He will also gather from every place, from the "ends of the earth ... ends of the heavens."

2.   What will be the reaction of the typical person to such a sight?

3.   What emotion does this picture bring to you … joy or fear?

In verse 28, Jesus returns to his own time and place. He resumes his use the personal pronoun "you." He also returns to the subject of "these things" (vs. 29, 30, 4, 8, 23).

The fig tree is probably mentioned because in Palestine most trees are evergreens. The rising of the sap in the fig tree's branches and the appearance of leaves is a sure sign that winter is over. In other words, just as the cycle of the tree is certain, the predictions of Jesus are certain.

24 But in those days, following that distress, "'the sun will be darkened, and the moon will not give its light; 25 the stars will fall from the sky, and the heavenly bodies will be shaken.' 26 At that time men will see the Son of Man coming in clouds with great power and glory. 27 And he will send his angels and gather his elect from the four winds, from the ends of the earth to the ends of the heavens. 28 Now learn this lesson from the fig tree: As soon as its twigs get tender and its leaves come out, you know that summer is near. 29 Even so, when you see these things happening, you know that it is near, right at the door. 30 I tell you the truth, this generation will certainly not pass away until all these things have happened. 31 Heaven and earth will pass away, but my words will never pass away.

My Thoughts Today …

What I Learned This Week …

… About Jesus

… About Ministry

… About Myself

Day 71
13:32-37

Day 72
14:1-2

Day 73
14:3-9

Day 74
14:10-11

Day 75
14:12-16

Week 11   The Opposition
Day 71-77   Mark 13:32-14:26

Day 76
14:17-21

Day 77
14:22-26

The Opposition

Mark 13:32–14:26

This week, as you walk with Jesus, he will tell his followers to "watch" and then he will spend the rest of the week watching his own back.

Sadly, the plots and attacks will come from within his own following. Notice how this makes the intimate setting of the Passover meal even more difficult and painful for Jesus.

Admire his courage. Follow his example.

My Prayer For This Week …

Read Mark 13:32-37

With very strong language, Jesus predicts that Jerusalem will fall within a "generation" (vs. 30). But with the same passion, he refuses to predict the end of the world, when "heaven and earth will pass away" (vs. 31). In fact, Jesus says "no one knows" (vs. 32).

The Angels Do Not Know — These heavenly workers rescue people (Ge 19:16; Da 6:22), battle evil (Ex 14:19), give directions and refreshment (Ex 23:20; Mk 1:13). They are a vital part of God's ministry on the earth (Heb 1:14). But, in spite of their special knowledge and "inside information" still they do not know when the end will come.

The Son Does Not Know — This might be difficult to comprehend. But remember Paul's description of Jesus. He writes that Jesus "emptied himself" (Php 2:7). In other words, he put himself under a self-imposed limitation. It was part of the price he paid to be one of us.

Only The Father Knows — Many religious leaders today will publish timetables and draw maps and charts detailing their calculated "day" when time will end. But how futile and arrogant for anyone today to claim to know what Jesus says only God knows.

1. Why didn't Jesus tell us the exact time that he would return?

2. How might a detailed outline of future events even hinder our faith?

When Jesus says that no one knows about "that day" he triggers thoughts and memories as old as the Old Testament prophets. In their writings the "Day of the Lord" was a description of God's work in the future (Joel 3:18; Am 8:3, 9, 13; 9:11; Mic 4:1-6; 7:4; 5:10; 7:11; Zep 1:9-10; 3:11, 16; Zec 9:16). These texts describe a future when God judges or rescues his people. And it will be followed by the last day. To prepare for the Last day, Jesus says to concentrate on the Present day. He says "watch". Those who are best prepared for the future are able to live fully today.

Be On Guard — This is the fourth warning Jesus has given in this chapter:

"Watch out that no one deceives you." (vs. 5)

"You must be on your guard. You will be handed over to the local councils." (vs. 9)

"So be on your guard; I have told you everything ahead of time." (vs. 23)

"Be on guard! Be alert! You do not know when that time will come." (vs. 33)

Always Watch — Using the illustration of the master leaving his home in the care of his servants, Jesus contrasts the faithful with the unfaithful. The faithful are always on duty, doing their job. Jesus uses the four Roman watches of the night (evening, midnight, before dawn, sunrise) to indicate that every moment (even the night) should be lived in view of that victorious future day.

3. What makes it difficult for you to watch and wait patiently?

Don't Fall Asleep — Jesus pictures the problem of passive waiting. Instead of working, this person is scanning the horizon looking for the master's return. Rather than follow a regular, steady course of action, his plan is to wait until the end is upon him before frantically rushing around in "last minute" preparation. The lesson is clear. The best preparation for the coming of our last day is to live today as if it were our last.

4. How can we "keep watch" even during our normal daily activities?

32 No one knows about that day or hour, not even the angels in heaven, nor the Son, but only the Father. 33 Be on guard! Be alert! You do not know when that time will come. 34 It's like a man going away: He leaves his house and puts his servants in charge, each with his assigned task, and tells the one at the door to keep watch. 35 Therefore keep watch because you do not know when the owner of the house will come back — whether in the evening, or at midnight, or when the rooster crows, or at dawn. 36 If he comes suddenly, do not let him find you sleeping. 37 What I say to you, I say to everyone: 'Watch!'"

My Thoughts Today …

Read Mark 14:1-2

Celebration … singing … family reunions … evening camp-fires covering the hills around the city. This is the mood of Jerusalem as Jesus' last days begin. It is a time of deeply felt emotions, story telling and festive family activities.

People Of Feasting — Passover is just one the many feasts observed yearly by the people of Israel. Three are required. In addition to the Passover there is the Feast of Pentecost and the Feast of Tabernacles. To these feasts every adult male Jew living within 15 miles of Jerusalem is required to come. But, in addition to the nearby residents, thousands more came from all over the Mediterranean world.

1. Imagine the feeling of excitement as people of common faith gather together in huge numbers. How would you feel to be a part of such an event?

2. Those who follow God have always been people of remembrance and celebration. What do we remember and celebrate in our assemblies and gatherings today?

One Feast Or Two? — The Feast of Passover and the Feast of Unleavened Bread occur together. Passover is observed on Nisan 14 (around April 14) and the Feast of Unleavened Bread is celebrated on the seven days that follow the Passover. Josephus reports that in AD 65, in response to emperor Nero's view that the Jewish religion was small and insignificant, a count was made of the number of lambs sold for Passover sacrifice (Jewish Wars 2. 14. 3). The Romans counted 265,000 sacrificial lambs. The minimum number for each group of pilgrims was ten persons per lamb. That year almost three million worshipers filled the city and surrounding country-side. Nero was astounded.

3. Read again the story of Israel's great escape in Exodus 12.

4. What kind of emotions must be flowing through a gathering this large?

Renewal And Reflection — Both feasts refresh ancient memories. Freedom. Escape. Deliverance. These are the themes being re-established and renewed in the heart of every Jew. In fact, everything is prepared in advance so this can be a time of reflection and decision. Roads and bridges are all repaired. All lodging is free. The city swells to overflowing with crowds of enthusiastic, happy people.

5. How would you describe the power of joy and commitment?

6. How does one person's joy and commitment feed another person's joy and commitment?

Deliverance Fever — But joy is not the only emotion running through the crowds. The festivity is mixed with tension. In fact, cries of celebration are often eclipsed by shouts of violence. Stories of the Old Deliverance from Egypt fuel the fires for a New Deliverance from Rome. The atmosphere is dangerously explosive. This is why any plan, on the part of the religious authorities, to openly stop Jesus must give way to a more secret or strategy.

7. What did many of the common people think of Jesus?

8. What is the advantage of a secret arrest over a public arrest?

9. Even though they lead in the festival, what is the true character of the Jewish leaders?

1 Now the Passover and the Feast of Unleavened Bread were only two days away, and the chief priests and the teachers of the law were looking for some sly way to arrest Jesus and kill him. 2 But not during the Feast," they said, "or the people may riot."

My Thoughts Today ...

Read Mark 14:3-9

It is Wednesday. Jesus does not go into Jerusalem. His days have been filled with public conflict, plots and anger. And so, here in the eye of his storm, he remains in the quietness of Bethany. For one whole day he rests with friends in peace and silence. In just a few hours he will walk back into the Holy City knowing that in this Passover, he will be the final sacrificial lamb. But rather than spend his last hours in fearful depression, Jesus attends a gathering of friends in the home of Simon the Leper.

Gratitude and Grief — Like many homes in Palestine, Simon's is built around an open courtyard where meals are eaten in warm weather. It is into this courtyard that a woman walks. John's story identifies her as Mary, probably the sister of Martha and Lazarus. Among Jesus' closest friends are Lazarus and his sisters. This would explain her twin motives of gratitude and grief.

Her Gratitude looks back to Jesus' many acts of kindness. But Her Grief looks forward to the growing hatred and hostility that surrounds Jesus. She seems to know what awaits him. And she knows that she has this one chance to give her gift. Her vial of potent perfume is meant to last for years, used one drop at a time. But in a moment of utter devotion, Mary gives it all. She seems to know that this opportunity will never come again.

1.   **Love doesn't always stop to calculate and measure. Why?**

2.   **What opportunities for love do you have today, but may not have tomorrow?**

Transforming Criticism — The disciples, including Judas (Jn 12:4) object to "this waste." Like most critics, they begin with principled criticism (the perfume), but then quickly move to personal criticism (the woman). As is often the case, criticism reveals more about the character of the critic than it does the one being criticized.

3.   **Criticism can be used to hurt or to heal. How can you be sure of your motive and your skill when you bring criticism to others?**

4.   **How should you respond when others rebuke your actions?**

A New Anointing — In the Old Testament, three kinds of people were anointed — Prophets who bring the word of God, Priests who build the bridge to God and Kings who lead the people for God.

5.   **How does Jesus fill all three roles?**

6.   **Which role touches you most deeply at this point in your life?**

But there is one more kind of person who is anointed … the dead. This is how Jesus understands Mary's gift. In fact, in order for the other three roles to come together, he must die.

The powerful fragrance of Mary's gift completely covers Jesus, permeating his clothes, drenching his hair and his beard. And as he moves through the next two days of shame, the aroma of Mary's honor will go with him. As he enters the upper room and walks through the garden. As he is led into the home of the high priest, and stands in both Herod's hall and Pilate's Praetorium. Even as he is nailed to the cross. Wherever he goes, Mary's devotion will go with him.

7.   **Mary gave without words. How can you give without words?**

3 While he was in Bethany, reclining at the table in the home of a man known as Simon the Leper, a woman came with an alabaster jar of very expensive perfume, made of pure nard. She broke the jar and poured the perfume on his head. 4 Some of those present were saying indignantly to one another, "Why this waste of perfume? 5 It could have been sold for more than a year's wages and the money given to the poor." And they rebuked her harshly. 6 "Leave her alone," said Jesus. "Why are you bothering her? She has done a beautiful thing to me. 7 The poor you will always have with you, and you can help them any time you want. But you will not always have me. 8 She did what she could. She poured perfume on my body beforehand to prepare for my burial. 9 I tell you the truth, wherever the gospel is preached throughout the world, what she has done will also be told, in memory of her."

My Thoughts Today ...

Read Mark 14:10-11

It is one the tragic ironies of this last Wednesday. On the very day that Mary pours out her love upon Jesus, Judas Iscariot takes steps to arrange his betrayal. It is the blending of these conflicting stories — the plot, the anointing and the betrayal that highlights both the beauty and the ugliness of each decision for or against Jesus.

A Nobel Name — The name Judas is a noble name going back to one the sons of Jacob who had been a hero in the hearts of the Jewish people for centuries. He produced David and Solomon and everyone expects the Messiah to come from his line.

After him another Judas (Judas Maccabaeus) had led a courageous rebellion against Israel's enemies in 164 BC. And while many others had failed, he succeeded in winning independence for his people. Since his story was also heroic many families gave their sons the name of this champion. In fact, by this time his name has become so common that Jesus has a brother named Judas and two of the twelve Apostles also wear the name Judas.

It is a heroic name in Jesus day, but not in our day. No one today would even dream of giving the name Judas to their child.

1.   What were Judas' parents hoping for him with the giving of his name?

2.   Judas "followed" Jesus earlier, why does he "betray" him now?

The "Can Do" Man — Earlier the chief priests had to delay their plot against Jesus (vs. 2). They were afraid of the crowds the feast had brought to Jerusalem. But Judas solves their problem. He tells them about the garden of Gethsemane and of Jesus' plans to be there. It is quiet. It is private and secluded. It is a good place to carry out their plot.

3.   Why are the chief priests "delighted" to hear Judas?

4.   In what ways can a Christian betray Jesus today?

5.   What situations today tempt Christians to compromise their faith?

Primed For Prompting — Just as Mary's anointing is a fitting prelude to Jesus' death (vs. 8), so also Judas' decision to betray Jesus matches the chief priest's murder plot. But how could Mary have known how the future would unfold? And how could Judas have foreseen of the evil intent of the chief priests? They were both prepared for their very different opportunities. But what primed them for their roles?

· For Mary — Her time with Jesus has been spent listening to his words and yielding to the influence for good in her life.

· For Judas — His time with Jesus has been spent resisting the influence for good in his life. As the one holding the money bag for the group he has helped himself to it frequently (Jn 12:6). In fact, this is probably why he complains so loudly about Mary's "waste" of expensive perfume.

· For Both — The qualities they allow into their lives shape their character and prime them for God's prompting for good (Mary) or Satan's prompting for evil (Judas — Jn 13:27).

6.   How can we open the door to God and close it to Satan?

10 Then Judas Iscariot, one of the Twelve, went to the chief priests to betray Jesus to them. 11 They were delighted to hear this and promised to give him money. So he watched for an opportunity to hand him over.

My Thoughts Today ...

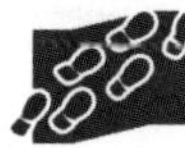

Read Mark 14:12-16

The Passover is a special holiday. It is a focal point of history and theology. It is the day Israel celebrates freedom. After 500 years of slavery to the Egyptians, God liberated His people. No more bricks. No more quotas. No more whips. Freedom.

The Setting — This story of deliverance began with God bringing ten plagues upon Egypt. Each successive plague added to the growing reason to let the Jews go. But only the horror of the final plague, the death of the first-born male, caused Pharaoh to finally concede. This is the victory that Jesus and the Twelve celebrate together. Moses left instructions for every family to celebrate the Passover, through each generation, as though they were the very ones being rescued from slavery that night. Jesus and his group are not from the same family, but still they celebrate this intimate family holiday.

1.   This feast was the setting for the first communion service. How can we bring this family focus to our communion service today?

2.   How do the themes of rescue and freedom tie the Passover story to the Cross story?

The Context — The Passover was celebrated with the closest friends and family. This makes Jesus' choice for this special table fellowship amazing. Sharing his last Passover are "friends" who will desert, deny and betray Jesus. He knows it is coming, he knows who will do it, and still he shares his bread with them all.

3.   How can Jesus share this time with those who will desert him?

4.   What power enables Him to stay with them?

5.   How can this same power enable you to share communion even with those who may have disappointed or hurt you?

The Structure — After cleaning the room, preparing the lamb and removing the leaven, Jesus and the Twelve gather around a horseshoe-shaped mat. Instead of standing at the feast as slaves, they recline on cushions, as free men. Four cups are mixed and drunk during the meal. Jesus takes the 3rd cup and gives it a new meaning. Three loaves of unleavened bread are normally used. Usually the middle loaf is broken and set aside for dessert. This is the loaf that Jesus characterizes in a new way. He is extending the meaning of the meal, something that has never been done before.

At the Exodus, to rescue his people from physical slavery, God sent plagues, opened the sea and became a pillar of fire. But now, to rescue his people from spiritual slavery, God becomes one of us, takes our place and pays our debt.

6.   What are your thoughts during communion each Sunday?

The Meaning —The bread is Jesus' body. The wine is His blood. He is the sacrificial lamb. And this is all so much more than a memory. It is a memorial. A memory looks back to an event in the past. But a memorial dramatically brings that event into the present as it empowers us to walk into our future.

7.   This next Sunday reflect on that sacrifice in the past, give thanks for the security of the present and request his power for the future.

Mark 14:12-16

12 On the first day of the Feast of Unleavened Bread, when it was customary to sacrifice the Passover lamb, Jesus' disciples asked him, "Where do you want us to go and make preparations for you to eat the Passover?" 13 So he sent two of his disciples, telling them, "Go into the city, and a man carrying a jar of water will meet you. Follow him. 14 Say to the owner of the house he enters, 'The Teacher asks: Where is my guest room, where I may eat the Passover with my disciples?' 15 He will show you a large upper room, furnished and ready. Make preparations for us there." 16 The disciples left, went into the city and found things just as Jesus had told them. So they prepared the Passover.

My Thoughts Today …

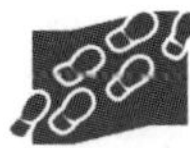

Read Mark 14:17-21

After all the planning and preparation, the actual feast time has finally come. For Jesus it is time to redefine its meaning. But for the Twelve, it is just another Passover. Of course, they probably find some of the preliminary instructions to be unusual. Following a man carrying a jar of water (vs. 13) is not their normal way of locating a suitable room. But they are used to receiving unusual instructions from Jesus.

Finally, the Passover evening has arrived and it seems that they are back on familiar ground. But are they?

Reclining At The Table — The first Passover had been celebrated standing. Of course it wasn't originally a celebration. It was a sign of haste as ancient Israel prepared for the Exodus, their flight from Egyptian slavery (Ex 12:11). It was not a leisurely meal of celebration. It was a hurried meal of escape. But, after centuries of use, it has become a sign of freedom and is always eaten reclining. The Jews have followed this procedure for centuries. It is all very predictable. That is, until tonight.

1.   **Tradition and custom was very important in Jesus' day.**

2.   **How powerful is it in today's typical church?**

3.   **How do Christians today react to changes in tradition?**

One Will Betray — Jesus and the Twelve have spent three years merging their very different ideas. They are an extremely diverse group and it has taken the wisdom and authority of Jesus himself to bring together all the divergent views and priorities. But while most of his group of followers are learning to yield and compromise, one is learning to hide.

4.   **Why is it that some are able to bend while others can only break?**

5.   **All the Apostles were flawed with problems, but Judas' flaw went deeper. How was it different? Why was it deeper?**

Eating With Me — Somehow Judas has been able to hide his developing agenda. Regardless of how pure his initial motives might have been, they have changed, becoming warped, evil and moving underground. Here at the supper, they are so hidden that he is able to play the dual role of faithful friend and faithless informant. No doubt Psalm 41:9 comes to Jesus' mind:

> *Even my close friend,*
> *whom I trusted,*
> *he who shared my bread,*
> *has lifted up his heel against me.*

6.   **Why do you think Jesus told his disciples that one of them would betray him without telling them his identity?**

7.   **Is he trying to protect Judas or send him one final message?**

8.   **What is his message for Judas?**

9.   **What is his message for us when, like Judas, we have the choice of faith or betrayal?**

17 When evening came, Jesus arrived with the Twelve. 18 While they were reclining at the table eating, he said, "I tell you the truth, one of you will betray me — one who is eating with me." 19 They were saddened, and one by one they said to him, "Surely not I?" 20 "It is one of the Twelve," he replied, "one who dips bread into the bowl with me. 21 The Son of Man will go just as it is written about him. But woe to that man who betrays the Son of Man! It would be better for him if he had not been born."

My Thoughts Today …

Read Mark 14:22-26

The prediction of betrayal (vs. 17-21) has changed the mood of the meal. It casts a discouraging shadow over all they are sharing. But it is an accurate shadow. It is the shadow of the cross.

1.   How does Jesus make betrayal a part of his Last Supper teaching?

The Passover meal has always been full of symbolism. Normally the elements of the meal on the table are used as object lessons to teach the meaning of the occasion. So, Jesus conforms to the atmosphere of the occasion by taking the bread and the cup as symbols and object lessons. The crucial difference is that he uses them, not to look back to the Exodus, but to look forward to his own death and to a new covenant.

2.   Do you prepare for your Lord's Supper experience? How?

It is important to remember the serious meaning of eating together in the ancient world. To share a meal means to establish or to confirm a relationship. This is why Jesus' leadership in this meal makes it a fellowship meal with him. He is the host. He is the leader and teacher. And so, he defines the terms:

The Bread (vs. 22) — As Jesus distributes the torn bread with the words "This is my body" he means, this is my person … this is my essence … this is all that I have said and done. And so, to share his bread, at his table, at his invitation, is to share his fate. We are joining ourselves to the purpose of his life and mission.

3.   How can you move your reflection on the Cross from a thankful communion moment to a renewed purpose for the coming week?

The Cup (vs. 23) — Jesus' mention of blood poured out is a Semitic way of describing a violent death (cf. Ge 4:10-11; 9:6; Dt 19:10; 2 Ki 21:16; Ps 106:38; Jer 7:6; Mt 23:35). He knows what is ahead. And soon everyone will know. So, for Jesus, the cup that he offers in symbol at the Supper, is the death that he will offer in reality on the Cross.

4.   It is clear what God offers in communion with you. What do you offer to God?

The Covenant (vs. 24) — In general terms this is a treaty between two parties. Usually such an agreement is sealed by the sacrifice of an animal and a little income from the two parties in the covenant. But the two parties in this covenant are Jesus and the "many" (vs. 24). There is no third party animal to lose his life and seal the agreement. Instead, this covenant will cost the "many" their commitment and Jesus his life. For us to share in his Cup each Sunday is to include ourselves in the "many" — the many who are saved, the many who are devoted, the many who are involved in his life and ministry.

5.   Are you one of the "many" who are saved? Are you one of the "many" who are involved and devoted?

The Hymn (vs. 26) — The Passover is usually concluded with the singing of the second half of the Hallel Psalms (chapters 115-118). They are great songs of praise to God. Perhaps for the Twelve this is just the traditional ending of the meal. But for Jesus, his praise in song will be matched and confirmed by his praise in a submitted life (cf. Lk 23:46).

6.   The next time you praise God in song from a comfortable pew, think how you will praise him later with a submitted life.

22 While they were eating, Jesus took bread, gave thanks and broke it, and gave it to his disciples, saying, "Take it; this is my body." 23 Then he took the cup, gave thanks and offered it to them, and they all drank from it. 24 "This is my blood of the covenant, which is poured out for many," he said to them. 25 "I tell you the truth, I will not drink again of the fruit of the vine until that day when I drink it anew in the kingdom of God." 26 When they had sung a hymn, they went out to the Mount of Olives.

My Thoughts Today ...

Week 11
What I Learned This Week …

… *About Jesus*

… *About Ministry*

… *About Myself*

Day 78
14:27-31

Day 79
14:32-42

Day 80
14:43-52

Day 81
14:53-65

Day 82
14:66-72

Day 83
15:1-5

Day 84
15:6-15

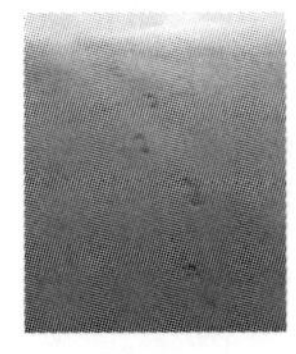

Week 12   The End
Day 78-84   Mark 14:27-15:15

The End

Mark 14:27-15:15

This week, as you walk with Jesus, watch him move from the anguish of the garden, to the violence of the arrest, to the pretense of the trial, on towards the agony of the cross. Notice that through it all, he continues to protect, serve, and teach the few who heard him then … and the millions who have heard him since.

Let his example inspire and teach you.

My Prayer For This Week …

Read Mark 14:27-31

It is late Thursday night or early Friday morning. After singing a final hymn, Jesus and his disciples leave the city. In the darkness they return to the Mount of Olives (vs. 26) where Jesus has often prayed (see Lk 22:39). The gospel of John adds the detail that Jesus crosses the Kidron Valley east of the city, just below the Temple itself. It is a winter stream, full of April rains. In fact, it is a natural drain for the city. The name "Kidron" means dusky, gloomy, murky — referring to the dark waters stained by the sacrificial blood from the Temple above. It is Passover time when Jesus steps across this dark stream and he knows that he is becoming the sacrificial lamb for the world.

John saw Jesus coming toward him and said, "Look, the Lamb of God, who takes away the sin of the world!
John 1:29
For Christ, our Passover lamb, has been sacrificed.
1 Corinthians 5:7
The precious blood of Christ, a lamb without blemish or defect.
1 Peter 1:19

1. **Imagine Jesus' thoughts as he crosses this valley of blood?**

2. **What power allows him to voluntarily walk into his own death?**

On the way, Jesus reveals a deep pain in his heart — the fact that he will face death alone. The swelling crowds that greeted him as he entered the city a few days ago (11:1-11) have steadily decreased in size. The fanfare of following him has lost its appeal. The controversy with the religious establishment has taken its toll. His firm teaching has made following him more difficult. Even his disciples will soon desert him.

3. **Why is it so difficult to face a painful moment alone?**

Scattered Sheep — The sobering fact is undeniable. Everyone will desert Jesus. Not only the crowds, not just some or most of his followers, but all of them. Judas has already made his treacherous move. But each of Jesus' trusted followers will eventually turn and run. Chaos will lead to confusion, which in turn, will lead to denial. Yes — the potential for unfaithfulness and cowardice is within us all.

4. **Why are these followers so unprepared for their own disloyalty?**

5. **What are the steps that lead to a denial of faith today?**

6. **Would it surprise you to see unfaithfulness grow in your own life?**

The Confidence Of Pride — Peter interrupts Jesus with pride. He is so sure that he puts himself above the others (vs. 29). It becomes a battle of pride versus truth. Notice the back and forth declarations:

> *Jesus (vs. 27) — "You will …"*
> *Peter (vs. 29) — "I will not …"*
> *Jesus (vs. 30) — "You yourself will …"*
> *Peter (vs. 31) — "I will never …"*

7. **What is the difference between confidence and pride?**

8. **What tests your loyalty to Christ? What strengthens your faith?**

27 You will all fall away," Jesus told them, "for it is written: "'I will strike the shepherd, and the sheep will be scattered.' 28 But after I have risen, I will go ahead of you into Galilee." 29 Peter declared, "Even if all fall away, I will not." 30 I tell you the truth," Jesus answered, "today — yes, tonight — before the rooster crows twice you yourself will disown me three times." 31 But Peter insisted emphatically, "Even if I have to die with you, I will never disown you." And all the others said the same.

My Thoughts Today …

Read Mark 14:32-42

The garden of Gethsemane is situated on the western slope, near the foot of the Mount of Olives. It is a special place for Jesus and his disciples. They have come here many times before (Mt 21:1; 24:3; Mk 11:1; 13:3; Lk 21:37; Jn 8:1). In the past it has been a place of peace and rest for Jesus. But this night, it will become a place of great suffering.

Famous Gardens — Gethsemane is one of three famous gardens in the Bible:

In the First Garden both human history and sin began. There in Eden, Adam's failure brought death to the human race.

Here in the Second Garden Jesus, the second Adam (1 Co 15:22, 45), answers the failure of the first garden. He brings life to the human race.

One day in the Third Garden death will die as "the river of the water of life" flows "from the throne of God and of the Lamb" (Rev 22:1).

The chronology of the gardens, the movement from death to life, hinges on what happens here in Gethsemane. This garden is the turning point of history.

1. What response does this turning point deserve?

Alone In The Garden — Eleven disciples follow their teacher into Gethsemane. Eight are asked to sit near the gate and pray. Three are singled out to go further. Peter, James and John have the privilege and the responsibility of seeing a preview of the cross. But even they are not taken into the deepest recesses of the garden. No one can go all the way with Jesus. Not one of us can bear the combined guilt of the human race — past, present and future. There is a point at which Jesus must goes alone.

2. Read these descriptions and write your reaction to the pain Jesus is feeling.

"Deeply distressed" (vs. 33) — Jesus is surprised, bewildered and astonished. What he sees in the future stuns and overwhelms him.

"Troubled" (vs. 33) — The basic meaning of this word is "to be away from home." Jesus was away from his home. He was away from his Father. And he will only move further away as he moves closer to the cross.

"Overwhelmed with sorrow to the point of death" (vs. 34) — Jesus has always been a man of sorrow. He has never been afraid to fully step into the pain of others. But here his pain is so great that everything in the past seems like tiny ripples compared to the waves that now break over and overwhelm him.

Two Wills — Read verse 36 again. Notice that Jesus mentions two wills. He contrasts "My will" and "Your will." In other words, this is a genuine decision, a real crisis. Jesus is really deciding whether to choose his will or his Father's will:

Jesus' Will — "Abba, Father . . . Take this cup from me."

The Father's Will — The cross and the salvation of humanity.

As before (1:35-39; 6:45-46), Jesus uses his time of prayer as a place to make a decision. He cries out to God. He listens to God. And in the strength of God, he makes his decision.

3. How does Jesus' courage affect your courage in times of crisis?

4. Use prayer now to made a decision of faith and courage.

32 They went to a place called Gethsemane, and Jesus said to his disciples, "Sit here while I pray." 33 He took Peter, James and John along with him, and he began to be deeply distressed and troubled. 34 My soul is overwhelmed with sorrow to the point of death," he said to them. "Stay here and keep watch." 35 Going a little farther, he fell to the ground and prayed that if possible the hour might pass from him. 36 Abba, Father," he said, "everything is possible for you. Take this cup from me. Yet not what I will, but what you will." 37 Then he returned to his disciples and found them sleeping. "Simon," he said to Peter, "are you asleep? Could you not keep watch for one hour? 38 Watch and pray so that you will not fall into temptation. The spirit is willing, but the body is weak." 39 Once more he went away and prayed the same thing. 40 When he came back, he again found them sleeping, because their eyes were heavy. They did not know what to say to him. 41 Returning the third time, he said to them, "Are you still sleeping and resting? Enough! The hour has come. Look, the Son of Man is betrayed into the hands of sinners. 42 Rise! Let us go! Here comes my betrayer!"

My Thoughts Today ...

Read Mark 14:43-52

It is difficult for Jesus to choose his Father's will because it will bring complete separation for the first time. But Jesus does what he has always done — he prays to a point of decision. He arises from prayer, wakes his disciples and meets his enemies. After so much emotional and spiritual pain in the garden it is amazing to watch Jesus now move with such confidence. As Judas arrives, Jesus steps out into the flickering light of the torches with such a composure that the armed crowd falls back in wonder and dismay (see Jn 18:1-6).

Caught From The Inside (vs. 43) — Notice that Judas is still listed as "one of the Twelve" — one of the chosen few, one of the hand-picked, one who heard all the teaching and saw all the wonders first hand. But still, one who is vulnerable to the plans and the attacks of Satan.

1.   What happens to our faith when pride convinces us that we are beyond temptation?

2.   How can we guard against this spiritual foolishness?

The Signal (vs. 44-45) — In Palestine, one man kissing another was a normal form of respectful greeting as in many cultures today. Here, Judas uses it to signal that Jesus is the one. Several motives can be driving this betrayal: jealousy, love of money, fear, disappointment, vindictiveness or all of the above. But, whatever the reasons, once they found a place in Judas' heart, Satan hardens them into action.

3.   What usually brings you to the point of moral or spiritual failure?

Religious Swords And Clubs (vs. 48-49) — The Sanhedrin does have a limited power of arrest. Therefore, with Judas as their guide, they make their move and the violence erupts. But amazingly, Jesus still acts with authority and power, even though he is the one to be arrested. He stops the violence, heals the wounded (Lk 22:51) and confronts his enemies. The scripture Jesus refers to (see vs. 27) is from Zechariah 13:7. The whole of 13:1-9 is the background for this stage of Jesus' life. It speaks of a time when God will provide a new cleansing from sin (13:1) and it refers to a blow against the "shepherd who is close to me" as a part of the process that will eventually lead to the creation of a new people of God (13:7-9).

4.   What can we learn from Jesus about facing opposition?

Everyone Deserted Him (vs. 50) — Jesus' followers (vs. 31) are thrown into a complete panic (see Jn 18:10), while he remains calm and confident. The difference can be traced back to the garden. There Jesus gave himself to intense preparation and prayer, while his disciples gave themselves to depression and sleep.

5.   What can Peter teach us about the wrong way to face opposition?

6.   How did Jesus' preparation for this moment give him his poise?

7.   Have you ever felt deserted? By how many? What did it feel like?

Naked Young Man (vs. 51-52) — It is only a guess that the young man who flees naked is Mark. At first, it seems to have no relevance to the story. But, since Mark is writing the story, it would be the kind of incident he would never forget and would feel compelled to record. Failure is often an unforgettable stain in our personal histories. But often it is also the turning point of decision and change.

8.   Reflect on those points of failure in your life which became points of decision and change. Can now be such a time?

43 Just as he was speaking, Judas, one of the Twelve, appeared. With him was a crowd armed with swords and clubs, sent from the chief priests, the teachers of the law, and the elders. 44 Now the betrayer had arranged a signal with them: "The one I kiss is the man; arrest him and lead him away under guard." 45 Going at once to Jesus, Judas said, "Rabbi!" and kissed him. 46 The men seized Jesus and arrested him. 47 Then one of those standing near drew his sword and struck the servant of the high priest, cutting off his ear. 48 Am I leading a rebellion," said Jesus, "that you have come out with swords and clubs to capture me? 49 Every day I was with you, teaching in the temple courts, and you did not arrest me. But the Scriptures must be fulfilled." 50 Then everyone deserted him and fled. 51 A young man, wearing nothing but a linen garment, was following Jesus. When they seized him, 52 he fled naked, leaving his garment behind.

My Thoughts Today ...

Mark 14:53-65

The enemies of Jesus will have to work fast if their plan is accomplished before the Sabbath. Every part of their plan has been carefully thought through. After being arrested, Jesus is quickly taken, first to the former high priest Annas (Jn 18:13-24) and then to his son-in-law Caiaphas, the current high priest. The news is spread that Jesus is in custody and the Sanhedrin is quickly and quietly called into a special meeting. Jesus is on trial, but this group is not really seeking truth and justice. They just want him dead. They eventually succeed, but along the way they also convict themselves of prejudice, dishonesty and hatred.

1.   What would drive a learned "religious" body of elders to become blind to their own principles of honesty, truth and mercy?

2.   Have you ever won your point but lost your honor?

As determined as they are to reach their goal of judicial murder, the Sanhedrin must still operate within the Roman system. In Judea, as in all the provinces of the empire, Rome gave the people a good measure of self-rule. But in cases involving the death penalty, Rome made the final judgment. So, the goal of this inquisition is to accuse Jesus of something which will successfully transfer into the Roman system. It doesn't matter what it is, as long as Jesus is executed. Here are the players in this drama:

Peter (vs. 54) — Everyone has deserted Jesus (vs. 50), but Peter does not run far. He seems to be forming and following a moment by moment plan. Tomorrow's study will describe each moment of Peter's uncertainty in painful detail.

3.   Why did Peter follow Jesus?

4.   Why did he follow at a distance?

Sanhedrin (vs. 55) — The Jewish court that gathers to listen to the accusations against Jesus is a group of seventy-one political and religious leaders from influential Jewish families — elders, lawyers, Pharisees and Sadducees. They are led by the high priest.

5.   What does this trial reveal about the character of the Sanhedrin?

High Priest (vs. 60-64) — It is a formal act for the high priest, to tear his clothes when a man is convicted of blasphemy. The tear has to be a specific length and only applied to specified clothes. Following his example, "they all condemned him" (vs. 64). Actually, they can not pass the sentence of death. But, with Jesus' confession that he is the Messiah, they now have something to convert into a political charge.

6.   How does it feel to be misinterpreted or misunderstood?

7.   With Jesus as your model how do you want to react the next time you are falsely accused?

Jesus (vs. 61-62) — Throughout this fraudulent trial, Jesus is calm and quiet (Isa 53:7; 1 Pe 2:23). Only at the end does he break his silence with the same words that earlier threw his captors to the ground in shock and amazement — "I am" (cf. Jn 18:5).

8.   What does Jesus teach us about the power of silence?

9.   What do you learn about his character from the trial?

53 They took Jesus to the high priest, and all the chief priests, elders and teachers of the law came together. 54 Peter followed him at a distance, right into the courtyard of the high priest. There he sat with the guards and warmed himself at the fire. 55 The chief priests and the whole Sanhedrin were looking for evidence against Jesus so that they could put him to death, but they did not find any. 56 Many testified falsely against him, but their statements did not agree. 57 Then some stood up and gave this false testimony against him: 58 We heard him say, 'I will destroy this man-made temple and in three days will build another, not made by man.'" 59 Yet even then their testimony did not agree. 60 Then the high priest stood up before them and asked Jesus, "Are you not going to answer? What is this testimony that these men are bringing against you?" 61 But Jesus remained silent and gave no answer. Again the high priest asked him, "Are you the Christ, the Son of the Blessed One?" 62 "I am," said Jesus. "And you will see the Son of Man sitting at the right hand of the Mighty One and coming on the clouds of heaven." 63 The high priest tore his clothes. "Why do we need any more witnesses?" he asked. 64 You have heard the blasphemy. What do you think?" They all condemned him as worthy of death. 65 Then some began to spit at him; they blindfolded him, struck him with their fists, and said, "Prophesy!" And the guards took him and beat him.

My Thoughts Today ...

Read Mark 14:66-72

This heart-rending and very personal episode was anticipated by Jesus (vs. 27-31) as it steadily moved from one painful step to another:

> *First is Peter's sleepy lack of concentration in Gethsemane (vs. 37).*
>
> *Next is his futile swordplay when the crowd comes to get Jesus (vs. 47; cf. Jn 18:10).*
>
> *Now we come to his half-hearted following (vs. 54).*

Peter is prepared to follow Jesus to the throne. He is ready to help restore Israel to political power. He is looking forward to taking his cabinet position on the "right" or "left" (cf. 10:35-41). But he isn't ready for this:

> *"Peter was below in the courtyard" (vs. 66)*

Peter is near but not with Jesus. Even in the face of his boasts (vs. 31), his fear and insecurity hold him at a distance (vs. 54). And Jesus does not force a closing of the gap. He does not call out Peter's name. Instead, he allows the distance. He only wants commitment when Peter chooses to give it.

1. What changed Peter from a bold defender to a distant follower?

> *"Peter (was) warming himself" (vs. 67).*

What is Peter doing? What would you be doing? He is thinking about what to do … unsure about which way to go. But how can he be indecisive after spending three years watching Jesus' power and compassion? The problem is that Peter began with his picture of Jesus already unalterably formed. So, the clearer Jesus becomes, the more frustrated Peter becomes (cf. 8:32).

2. What kinds of things are going through Peter's mind as he sits and thinks?

> *"He denied it" (vs. 68)*
>
> *"Again he denied it" (vs. 70)*
>
> *"He began to call down curses … I don't know this man" (vs. 71)*

The natural course of indecision is decision by default. Unlike Jesus, Peter has not prepared for this crisis. At every fork in the road, Jesus has chosen God's way. The accumulated godly decisions have prepared him for this crisis. Peter accumulated an indecisive style. And so, when pushed, he denies.

3. Why are Christians often afraid to talk openly about their faith?

> *"Peter remembered" (vs. 72)*

What is it that Peter remembers? Initially he remembers Jesus' words about the rooster. But what else does he remember? Does he remember Jesus' constant commitment to him? Does he remember being a part of Jesus' ministry … the healings … the feedings … the miracles? There is one line from Jesus he should remember — (vs. 28) "But after I have risen, I will go ahead of you into Galilee."

4. Look back on your own relationship with Jesus. What do you remember? What do you see?

> *"He broke down and wept" (vs. 72)*

He is very sorry. But, at this point, he still cannot take his stand with Jesus. He does not retract all of his denials. Instead, he goes outside to cry (see Lk 22:62).

5. Read 1 Co 7:8-11. Of the two kinds of sorrows described, which do you usually experience?

66 While Peter was below in the courtyard, one of the servant girls of the high priest came by. 67 When she saw Peter warming himself, she looked closely at him. "You also were with that Nazarene, Jesus," she said. 68 But he denied it. "I don't know or understand what you're talking about," he said, and went out into the entryway. 69 When the servant girl saw him there, she said again to those standing around, "This fellow is one of them." 70 Again he denied it. After a little while, those standing near said to Peter, "Surely you are one of them, for you are a Galilean." 71 He began to call down curses on himself, and he swore to them, "I don't know this man you're talking about." 72 Immediately the rooster crowed the second time. Then Peter remembered the word Jesus had spoken to him: "Before the rooster crows twice you will disown me three times." And he broke down and wept.

My Thoughts Today …

Read Mark 15:1-5

After being held somewhere in the palace of Caiaphas from about three o'clock until daybreak, Jesus is taken "very early in the morning" (vs. 1) to another meeting. One possible reason for this second meeting is to give some semblance of legality to the plan of action against Jesus. But, any display of legality will be difficult to see considering the many violations of Jewish regulations that have already taken place. For example:

Capital Cases can be tried only during the day and only in the regular meeting place in the temple, the Hewn Chamber (see 14:53-54).

A Conviction can not be pronounced on the first day of a trial. Only a verdict of "not guilty" can be reached on the first day. Jesus is found guilty and abused, not only on the first day, but also during the first session of the first day (see 14:56-64)

Court Proceedings cannot be conducted on Sabbath days or feast days.

Voting must begin with the youngest members of the Sanhedrin so that the junior members will not be influenced by the senior members (see 14:63).

Witnesses must be examined separately with an elaborate system of warning and cautioning. Their testimony must agree in every detail to be valid.

1.   **Describe the power of a group. How does Jesus react to this group?**

2.   **How do you usually react to the power of a group?**

The "decision" reached is no surprise. Early in the story (3:6) the goal to kill Jesus was decided. Now that their goal is in sight, they move to the next stage. They take Jesus to the one person who can carry out the death sentence — Pilate.

His History — In 1961 a stone slab was discovered at Caesarea bearing the name Pontius Pilatus. Tacitus refers to the execution of Jesus by Pilate and two Jewish writers, Philo and Josephus, describe Pilate as harsh and brutal in his dealings with the Jews.

His Rank — Pilate is not a highborn Roman. He has a middle rank having served in the army. While in Rome he married into a very important Roman family. Claudia Procula was the daughter of the Emperor Tiberus and the granddaughter of Caesar Augustus. These connections helped Pilate to move up. In AD 26 he was appointed procurator of Judea. Because of his family connections he was allowed the unusual privilege of taking his wife with him to Judea. Luke 3:1 reports that Pilate was governor when John the Baptist began his ministry.

His Job — Procurator is not normally a top appointment, but in Judea it carries more responsibility. Pilate is responsible for upholding law and order, administering justice and collecting taxes. But he goes about his duties in a coarse, tactless and offensive way. For four years prior to meeting Jesus, Pilate has bungled one crisis after another. His self-justifying attitude has left him morally paralyzed, afraid to act. He is as unprepared for this meeting as Jesus is prepared.

3.   **Contrast the two men who now face each other — Pilate and Jesus.**

4.   **Whom do today's social and political leaders most resemble?**

5.   **Which kind of "leadership" model impresses you the most? Why?**

1 Very early in the morning, the chief priests, with the elders, the teachers of the law and the whole Sanhedrin, reached a decision. They bound Jesus, led him away and handed him over to Pilate. 2 Are you the king of the Jews?" asked Pilate. "Yes, it is as you say," Jesus replied. 3 The chief priests accused him of many things. 4 So again Pilate asked him, "Aren't you going to answer? See how many things they are accusing you of." 5 But Jesus still made no reply, and Pilate was amazed.

My Thoughts Today …

Read Mark 15:6-15

The irony of the charge against Jesus is staggering. He is charged with treason. He is accused of trying to seize political power. There is no doubt that he is the king of the Jews in a spiritual sense. But, over and over he has refused every political opportunity (see 6:30-46; Jn 6:15). But amazingly, he is still, charged with blasphemy and treason.

1. Why doesn't Jesus speak up and try to correct the misrepresentation about him?

2. How can he be so calm and confident?

Pilate — The Jewish court expects Pilate to rubber-stamp their decision. But his wife dreams about Jesus and sends the message, "Don't have anything to do with that innocent man, because I have suffered a great deal today in a dream on account of him" (Mt 27:19). And so Pilate faces a dilemma. He can either disappoint the Jews, cause a riot and report another failure to Rome, or he can disappoint his wife, a relative of the emperor. Pilate decides to follow his wife's advice. And so, when the Jews arrive, instead of confirming their plan, he unexpectedly asks, "What charges are you bringing against this man" (Jn 18:29). He wants no part of this. He even tries to pass Jesus on to Herod, who is visiting from Galilee (Lk 23:6-11), but it doesn't work. Herod sends Jesus back. Pilate even tries to call upon an old tradition and release Jesus because of the feast. But even this doesn't work.

3. How would you feel if you were the judge of Jesus?

4. Why did Pilate try to release Jesus? Why didn't it work?

Barabbas — The name Barabbas is a combination of two words. Bar means "a son." Abbas means "a father." Together they mean "a son of a father." This is not an extremely significant detail until we consider Pilate's other choice of who to release — Jesus, The Son of The Father. The practice of releasing prisoners at a religious feast was common in Babylonian, Assyrian, Greek and Roman cultures. In fact, one recipient of a Babylonian reprieve was Jehoiachin, king of Judah. He was freed in 561 BC (2 Ki 25:27-30; Jer 52:31-34). Many cultures released prisoners during religious festivals, at new year's celebrations and on other occasions. But never has the choice been more crucial than on this Friday morning.

5. Put yourself in the place of Barabbas …

First — How would you feel as you face your imminent death by crucifixion?

Second — How would you feel as the guards open your cell to release you?

The Crowd — Throughout Jesus' ministry the crowds have been shifting from support to opposition. With typical instability they have moved from being amazed by Jesus in the beginning, to using Jesus for a meal or a trick, to finally killing Jesus today.

6. What makes it difficult to step out of the crowd and stand alone in our faith?

During all the interplay among the angry, confused people in this story, we see Jesus, calm, dignified and in control. Pilate can find nothing wrong with him. But instead of courageously acting on his heart, he washes his hands (Mt 27:24) and steps out of the picture.

7. Why is it impossible to be neutral about Jesus?

8. Where do you stand today?

6 Now it was the custom at the Feast to release a prisoner whom the people requested. 7 A man called Barabbas was in prison with the insurrectionists who had committed murder in the uprising. 8 The crowd came up and asked Pilate to do for them what he usually did. 9 Do you want me to release to you the king of the Jews?" asked Pilate, 10 knowing it was out of envy that the chief priests had handed Jesus over to him. 11 But the chief priests stirred up the crowd to have Pilate release Barabbas instead. 12 What shall I do, then, with the one you call the king of the Jews?" Pilate asked them. 13 Crucify him!" they shouted. 14 Why? What crime has he committed?" asked Pilate. But they shouted all the louder, "Crucify him!" 15 Wanting to satisfy the crowd, Pilate released Barabbas to them. He had Jesus flogged, and handed him over to be crucified.

My Thoughts Today ...

What I Learned This Week ...

... *About Jesus*

... *About Ministry*

... *About Myself*

Day 85
15:16-20

Day 86
15:21-32

Day 87
15:33-41

Day 88
15:42-47

Day 89
16:1-8

Day 90
16:9-20

Week 13   The Victory
Day 85-90   Mark 15:16-16:20

The Victory

Mark 15:16-16:20

This week, as you walk with Jesus, hear him utter his amazing "Last Words" while hanging on the cross. Notice how the spectacle of his death brings new bold-ness to a "secret" disciple. Prepare yourself to see how his resurrection will change the course of history.

Reflect on the power of your own decision to follow Jesus in your own death, burial, and resurrection.

My Prayer For This Week …

Read Mark 15:16-20

Amazingly Jesus allows himself to be "led away." Through the next two days, he will permit himself to be led from one place and one person to another. The exhausting back and forth trips are part of the debt of the human race. It all brings to mind the ancient prophecy from Isaiah 53:7 —

"He was led like a lamb to the slaughter."

On Thursday Jesus is led ...

	Matthew	Mark	Luke	John
To Annas				18:12-14
To Caiaphas	26:57-68	14:53-65	22:54-65	18:24

On Friday Jesus is led ...

	Matthew	Mark	Luke	John
To Pilate	27:2, 11-14	15:1-5	23:1-5	18:28-38
To Herod			23:6-12	
To Pilate	27:15-26		23:13-25	
Inside the Praetorium	27:27-30	15:16-19		18:33-19:4
Outside before the crowds				19:5-8
Inside the Praetorium			19:9-12	
Outside before the crowds				19:13-16
To the Cross	27:31-56	15:20-41	23:26-49	19:17-37

The Roman practice of crucifixion involves so much more than just nailing a person to a cross to die. It also includes the absolute humiliation and unrestrained torture of that person. It's no wonder that crucifixion is the horror of the ancient world.

1. When have you been ridiculed for your faith? How does it feel to be mocked by others?

2. What can we learn from Jesus about suffering for our faith?

Compare this punishment with the Jewish trial earlier. There are similarities. In both Jesus is ridiculed, spat upon and beaten. But there are also important differences:

The Jews are driven by hatred. They cannot accept Jesus as a prophet with divine power. They blindfold him, hit him with their fists and say, in effect, "If you are a prophet from God, guess who hit you" (14:65).

Pilate is driven by cowardice, and so the Jews carefully make this a political concern. Among the charges against Jesus is his claim to be "King of the Jews" (15:2, 18). Pilate has mishandled the Jews many times before. He really wants no part of this problem and eventually washes his hands of it (Mt 27:24).

The Soldiers are driven by cruelty. To them, Jesus is just another execution. So, why not add a little fun to a routine job?

3. How are Christians treated today in your social setting?

4. What should be your response when your faith is criticized?

5. How can you encourage other believers who suffer for their faith?

16 The soldiers led Jesus away into the palace (that is, the Praetorium) and called together the whole company of soldiers. 17 They put a purple robe on him, then twisted together a crown of thorns and set it on him. 18 And they began to call out to him, "Hail, king of the Jews!" 19 Again and again they struck him on the head with a staff and spit on him. Falling on their knees, they paid homage to him. 20 And when they had mocked him, they took off the purple robe and put his own clothes on him. Then they led him out to crucify him.

My Thoughts Today …

Read Mark 15:21-32

After he appears before Pilate and is ridiculed by the Roman soldiers, Jesus is taken from the Fortress Antionia to the place of execution outside the city. By design this is a public execution. Therefore, Jesus carries his own instrument of torture — the cross-beam (Jn 19:17). The occupying Romans want their "justice" to be clearly seen and feared by everyone. But after being marched around the city all night, with brutal treatment at each stop, Jesus is already exhausted and cannot continue.

A Certain Man (vs. 21) — Imagine traveling an extended distance from your home in Cyrene, Africa to celebrate Passover in the holy city of Jerusalem. This has been the ambition of Simon since the day he first began to plan his trip. But as he enters the city, he is "forced" to carry the cross of a stranger.

1.   How would it feel to have your life-long plans ruined in this way?

There is one reason for Mark to mention Simon's sons Rufus and Alexander. They were probably known by his readers (see Ro 16:13). Simon probably did more than simply carry Jesus' cross that day. He eventually carried his own in discipleship.

2.   What does it mean to take up our cross to follow Jesus today (cf. 8:34)?

A Drugged Wine (vs. 23) — Before crucifixion, Jesus is offered a crude narcotic to help him endure the pain. It is the only offer of mercy extended. He tastes the potion and then refuses to cloud his senses and dull his pain. He chooses to fully experience the cross.

3.   Why does Jesus choose to fully experience this ordeal?

A Slave's Death (vs. 25) — Even criminals, who are Roman citizens, are spared the horror and humiliation of crucifixion. It is reserved for the lowest class. It is a slave's death, offensive and obscene in every way. One major purpose of crucifixion, is to display the accused. In fact, often the person hung on a cross is already dead. The point is to shame the criminal and communicate that message of shame to everyone who passes by.

4.   What does Jesus teach you about suffering for your faith?

A Confusing Charge (vs. 26) — Above the head of Jesus, is nailed the titulus, a board that spells out the charge against him. It says "The King of the Jews." This is the placard he wore as he walked to the place of execution. It is placed on the cross, much to the dismay of the Jewish leaders (see Jn 19:19-22). The irony of this sign is that its purpose is to charge Jesus with a crime. But, in fact, its charge is true. He is the King.

5.   Define what it means for Jesus to be king in your life today.

A Mocking Truth (vs. 31-32) — How ironic are the words taunting Jesus, "He saved other … but he can't save himself." Their taunt is true! Jesus had said, "For even the Son of Man did not come to be served, but to serve, and to give his life as a ransom for many" (10:45). There is no doubt that he can end his suffering any time and answer the mockery by coming, "down now from the cross" (vs. 32). He can save himself, but only by abandoning his mission and us. The chief priests and teachers of the law say they will believe Jesus if he comes down from the cross. But we believe in him because he remained on the cross.

6.   How has your understanding of Jesus' cross grown or changed?

21 A certain man from Cyrene, Simon, the father of Alexander and Rufus, was passing by on his way in from the country, and they forced him to carry the cross. 22 They brought Jesus to the place called Golgotha (which means The Place of the Skull). 23 Then they offered him wine mixed with myrrh, but he did not take it. 24 And they crucified him. Dividing up his clothes, they cast lots to see what each would get. 25 It was the third hour when they crucified him. 26 The written notice of the charge against him read: THE KING OF THE JEWS. 27 They crucified two robbers with him, one on his right and one on his left. 29 Those who passed by hurled insults at him, shaking their heads and saying, "So! You who are going to destroy the temple and build it in three days, 30 come down from the cross and save yourself!" 31 In the same way the chief priests and the teachers of the law mocked him among themselves. "He saved others," they said, "but he can't save himself! 32 Let this Christ, this King of Israel, come down now from the cross, that we may see and believe." Those crucified with him also heaped insults on him.

My Thoughts Today ...

Read Mark 15:33-41

No gospel writer spends much time describing the details of crucifixion. Like Mark, they simply record that "they crucified him" (see Mt 27:35; Lk 23:33; Jn 19:18). But together, they preserve the most remarkable statements ever made by a dying man.

Mercy — "Father, forgive them" (Lk 23:34). Jesus doesn't curse those around him (cf. Mk 15:32). He doesn't appeal to his innocence or talk incoherently like a mad man. Instead, he prays for those killing him. What Jesus is really saying is, "Father, forgive them and condemn me."

1.   How have you responded to his mercy?

Compassion — "I tell you the truth, today you will be with me" (Lk 23:43). Jesus has always been interrupted … his sleep, his meals, his teaching. And now, even his dying prayer is interrupted by a desperate thief. The thief has no illusions. He has no answers. He just wants help. To the taunts of the crowd Jesus gave no answer. But the plea of this remorseful man drew an immediate response — "Today you will be with me." Compassion was his work.

2.   When were you last at the point of desperation?

3.   What brought you there?

4.   What can bring you there now?

Devotion — "Here is your son … here is your mother" (Jn 19:26-27) So absorbed in suffering, so preoccupied in bearing the combined guilt of the whole world, it seems that Jesus could easily forget family ties. But he doesn't. The widow … the orphan … even on the cross, he thinks of others.

5.   In your own times of suffering, with whom are you most concerned?

Isolation — "My God, my God, why have you forsaken me" (Mk 15:34) Until now, Jesus has been abandoned by his disciples, by the religious establishment and by most of his friends and family. But to truly bear the punishment of the guilty he must also be abandoned by God. Now he is completely alone as he experiences every pain and all suffering ancient and modern. This sixth hour is the climax of his crisis.

6.   Write, in your own words, why Jesus had to be abandoned by God.

Agony — "I am thirsty" (Jn 19:28). Here spiritual agony and physical agony touch. Is Jesus just thirsting for water (see Ps 22:15) or is he thirsting for God (see Ps 63:1)? A soldier offers a sponge of sour wine. With his throat partially soothed, Jesus is ready to speak two final statements.

Completion — "It is finished" (Jn 19:30). This is a statement of victory as Jesus reaches his goal and finishes his work. He transforms the meaning of the cross from an ancient instrument of torture into a timeless vehicle of salvation.

7.   Reflect on your own baptism — the place where you touch His cross (see Ro 6:1-7).

Conviction — "Father, into your hands I commit my spirit" (Lk 23:46). These words are a prayer from Psalm 31 and the everyday prayer of the Jewish people. And with them, he is gone, confidently placing himself in his Father's hands. Following his Father's plan.

8.   How would you describe the level of your confidence in God's leadership?

Mark 15:33-41

33 At the sixth hour darkness came over the whole land until the ninth hour. 34 And at the ninth hour Jesus cried out in a loud voice, "Eloi, Eloi, lama sabachthani?"—which means, "My God, my God, why have you forsaken me?" 35 When some of those standing near heard this, they said, "Listen, he's calling Elijah." 36 One man ran, filled a sponge with wine vinegar, put it on a stick, and offered it to Jesus to drink. "Now leave him alone. Let's see if Elijah comes to take him down," he said. 37 With a loud cry, Jesus breathed his last. 38 The curtain of the temple was torn in two from top to bottom. 39 And when the centurion, who stood there in front of Jesus, heard his cry and saw how he died, he said, "Surely this man was the Son of God!" 40 Some women were watching from a distance. Among them were Mary Magdalene, Mary the mother of James the younger and of Joses, and Salome. 41 In Galilee these women had followed him and cared for his needs. Many other women who had come up with him to Jerusalem were also there.

My Thoughts Today . . .

Read Mark 15:42-47

Neither Pilate nor the Sanhedrin have any intention of giving Jesus anything that even resembles an honorable burial. After all, he has not died with honor. That is the point of having him crucified. The motive behind their plan to kill Jesus has always been very clear. But not so clear is what they plan to do with the body. Often crucifixion victims are never buried as a further dishonor. But because of the approaching Sabbath, something must be done with the body, if only to avoid defiling the land.

If a man guilty of a capital offense is put to death and his body is hung on a tree,
you must not leave his body on the tree overnight.
Be sure to bury him that same day,
because anyone who is hung on a tree is under God's curse.
You must not desecrate the land the LORD your God is giving you as an inheritance.
Deuteronomy 21:22-23

We will never know what the Sanhedrin might have done because a "secret disciple" (see Jn 19:38) Joseph of Arimathea steps forward to claim Jesus' body. Joseph wants to bury Jesus in his own new tomb.

A Council Member — Joseph is mentioned in all four gospels in connection with the burial of Jesus. He is a rich man (Mt 27:57). He is a respected member of the Sanhedrin (Mk 15:43). He is a good man who did not approve of all that has been happening to Jesus (Lk 23:50-51).

1.   As a council member, what might he have seen that would bother him?

A Secret Disciple — Joseph is a disciple of Jesus, but until now, he has been a fearful disciple. He isn't afraid of Jesus. Jesus is the attraction. He is afraid of the reaction of others. So, until now, he has kept his discipleship a secret.

2.   Today, with our religious freedom, why do many hide their faith?

A Changed Man — Along with another secret disciple, fellow council member Nicodemus (see Jn 3:1ff; 19:38-42), Joseph undergoes a dramatic change. Something begins to pull both of them out of their secrecy. Something powerful has happened that is bringing maturity and courage to their faith. The single event that is changing their discipleship is the cross of Jesus.

There they see His Purpose and how far He will go to accomplish it.

There they see His Love for humanity, both friend and enemy alike.

There they see the Injustice of the cross and it tears them loose. They are no longer afraid, no longer hidden, no longer secret disciples. Instead, they are open, vocal and public. Remember Jesus' words:

But I, when I am lifted up from the earth, will draw all men to myself.
John 12:32

3.   What tempts you the most to take your discipleship underground?

4.   What would drive "secret disciples" out of their secrecy today?

5.   What does mean to "boldly" live out the Christian faith today?

6.   What is the difference between boldness and arrogance?

Mark 15:42-47

42 It was Preparation Day (that is, the day before the Sabbath). So as evening approached, 43 Joseph of Arimathea, a prominent member of the Council, who was himself waiting for the kingdom of God, went boldly to Pilate and asked for Jesus' body. 44 Pilate was surprised to hear that he was already dead. Summoning the centurion, he asked him if Jesus had already died. 45 When he learned from the centurion that it was so, he gave the body to Joseph. 46 So Joseph bought some linen cloth, took down the body, wrapped it in the linen, and placed it in a tomb cut out of rock. Then he rolled a stone against the entrance of the tomb. 47 Mary Magdalene and Mary the mother of Joses saw where he was laid.

My Thoughts Today …

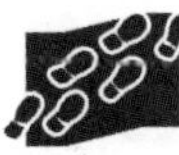

Read Mark 16:1-8

Put yourself in this group of disciples who have been following Jesus for three years. Imagine how you are feeling. Consider all you have been through. In just the past few days you have experienced:

Death — A close friend is murdered.

Insecurity — All you have been building is falling apart.

Hopelessness — Your dreams for the future are all gone.

Isolation — Your brotherhood of close friends is breaking up.

Disappointment — The cause you have believed in is turning sour.

Suicide — One of your friends hangs himself.

Betrayal — You feel let down by the one person in the world you trusted.

Shame — Everyone in the community thinks you have wasted your life.

1.   How would you handle these feelings of defeat?

2.   What would you need to restore your confidence?

On Sunday, after the Sabbath restrictions have passed, three women bring spices intending to re-wrap and anoint Jesus' body. But they are worried and uncertain. A military guard has been placed at the tomb and an official seal put on the stone. Will they be allowed near the tomb? Who will roll away the massive stone?

Their concern is very valid. As a political and religious figure, Jesus is a problem to both the Romans and the Jews. Even the possibility of his resurrection is a political and religious time bomb! So, consider the security precautions that have been taken:

The Death (Mk 15:39, 44-45) — Scourging. Shock. Loss of blood. Asphyxiation. There is no doubt in the minds of these professional killers that Jesus is dead.

The Preparation (Mk 15:46) — Jesus body is washed, wrapped and anointed with 75 pounds of a thick, glue-like spice.

The Burial (Mk 15:46; Jn 19:41-42) — This is a new tomb, cut out of solid rock. There is no back door and no way to dig out.

The Stone (Mk 16:4; Mt 27:60) — A groove is cut so that its lowest point lay just in front the opening to the tomb. A "very large" stone (vs. 4) is rolled into place covering the opening.

The Guard And Seal (Mt 27:62-66) — Because of the political and religious turmoil both the Romans and the Jews want Jesus to stay in the tomb.

And so, when the women arrive at the tomb, imagine their surprise to find the Roman seal broken, the guards AWOL, the stone rolled away and the tomb empty. No one saw his resurrection. It was as unobserved as Mary's conception. But just as the plan of God put him in the womb, and just as the love of God took him to the cross, now the power of God raises him from the dead. In one swift moment everything changed. The young man's message (vs. 5-7) fills the women with fear and excitement.

He has risen! He is not here. Go tell his disciples

3.   How would you react? What would you do?

4.   Where would you go? Who would you tell first?

Mark 16:1-8

1 When the Sabbath was over, Mary Magdalene, Mary the mother of James, and Salome bought spices so that they might go to anoint Jesus' body. 2 Very early on the first day of the week, just after sunrise, they were on their way to the tomb 3 and they asked each other, "Who will roll the stone away from the entrance of the tomb?" 4 But when they looked up, they saw that the stone, which was very large, had been rolled away. 5 As they entered the tomb, they saw a young man dressed in a white robe sitting on the right side, and they were alarmed. 6 Don't be alarmed," he said. "You are looking for Jesus the Nazarene, who was crucified. He has risen! He is not here. See the place where they laid him. 7 But go, tell his disciples and Peter, 'He is going ahead of you into Galilee. There you will see him, just as he told you.'" 8 Trembling and bewildered, the women went out and fled from the tomb. They said nothing to anyone, because they were afraid.

My Thoughts Today ...:

Read Mark 16:9-20

The angel says that Jesus is going to Galilee (vs. 7). It was in Jerusalem that Jesus spoke of a final Galilee experience (see 14:27-28). And so, after the tragedy of Jerusalem, he returns to that place where ministry began. He reassembles his scattered flock. He wants them to connect the excitement of their first Galilee encounter with the power of their last — Resurrection. In the beginning, Galilee had been a place of preparation. Here at the end, it becomes the springboard of mission.

The Messengers — After appearing to hundreds of His followers, "Jesus appeared to the Eleven" (vs. 14). In fact, the Commission is directed "to them" (vs. 15). Because of this, some have mistakenly concluded that this mission is theirs alone. After all, they are the eye-witnesses. They are the specially trained disciples. They are especially equipped to be the messengers. Today this mentality shows itself in a clergy/laity separation. Some even say, "I'm not a trained minister. Leave ministry to the professionals." The assumption is that the Eleven are highly trained professionals, ready to pick up where Jesus left off. But are they?

1. Think back through the last 90 days (esp. 8:18, 33; 14:27, 50; 16:11, 14). List the common ground we all share with the Twelve.

2. How do you see your own personal role as a messenger for Jesus?

The Mission — Sending the Eleven into the world with the most important mission ever given might seem to be a curious cure for a "lack of faith" and a "stubborn refusal to believe" (vs. 14). But they are not only learning to trust in God's power, they are also learning to relinquish their own agenda. The failure of their own mission has opened their eyes. Now they can see what Jesus has been teaching and modeling for them all along. He deals with them individually (Jn 20:24-29; 21:15-19) and as a group (Mt 28:16) entrusting his mission to them. He says preach the good news (Mk 16:15), baptize and teach (Mt 28:19-20), make disciples (Mt 28:19) and feed my sheep (Jn 21:17).

3. How has your own agenda blinded you to God's mission?

4. How has God used your failure as the beginning of his ministry?

The Message — This 90-Day Study begins and ends with the term "gospel" or "good news" (Mk 1:1, 14; 16:15). This is the message the Apostles are to take to the world. Framed by this good-news terminology is the good news itself. The "news" is the story of Jesus. This sounds too simple. But we must not assume that the news about Jesus is already known. The "news" is so important that the New Testament contains four accounts. We must be certain to leave the "news" about Jesus in the Gospel that we preach.

What makes his news "good" is the resurrection. Only his story has an ending we can truly live with.

5. What happens to our message if the story of Jesus is left out?

6. What are people responding to, if not to Jesus?

We should not be surprised, as we read the story, that so many respond to the "good news" in faith and baptism (Mk 16:16; Ac 2:38, 41). The "news" about Jesus is that "good."

9 When Jesus rose early on the first day of the week, he appeared first to Mary Magdalene, out of whom he had driven seven demons. 10 She went and told those who had been with him and who were mourning and weeping. 11 When they heard that Jesus was alive and that she had seen him, they did not believe it. 12 Afterward Jesus appeared in a different form to two of them while they were walking in the country. 13 These returned and reported it to the rest; but they did not believe them either. 14 Later Jesus appeared to the Eleven as they were eating; he rebuked them for their lack of faith and their stubborn refusal to believe those who had seen him after he had risen. 15 He said to them, "Go into all the world and preach the good news to all creation. 16 Whoever believes and is baptized will be saved, but whoever does not believe will be condemned. 17 And these signs will accompany those who believe: In my name they will drive out demons; they will speak in new tongues; 18 they will pick up snakes with their hands; and when they drink deadly poison, it will not hurt them at all; they will place their hands on sick people, and they will get well." 19 After the Lord Jesus had spoken to them, he was taken up into heaven and he sat at the right hand of God. 20 Then the disciples went out and preached everywhere, and the Lord worked with them and confirmed his word by the signs that accompanied it.

My Thoughts Today ...

... About Jesus

… About Ministry

… About Myself